Common-Sense Fly Fishing

Common-Sense
Fly Fishing

7 Simple Lessons to Catch More Trout

By Eric Stroup

Foreword by Charles Meck
Illustrations by Dave Hall

HEADWATER
BOOKS

Published by

HEADWATER BOOKS
531 Harding Street
New Cumberland, PA 17070
www.headwaterbooks.com

Illustrations by Dave Hall
Book design by Ryan Scheife, Mayfly Design

Printed in United States of America

First edition

10 9 8 7 6 5 4 3 2 1

ISBN: 978-1-934753-07-1

Library of Congress Control Number: 2009939818

This book is dedicated to the brave men and women who have sacrificed everything for our freedom, and for all who serve in our Armed Forces protecting and defending our way of life. May God bless you.

Contents

Acknowledgments

When I think of all the people that have influenced the development of my fishing career, I have to thank the most recent addition first. My wife, Tracey, is the single most positive influence I have ever had in my life. She is the most supportive and loving partner a fisherman could have, and she has inspired me to become a better person. This book is a product of her support, inspiration, and encouragement.

I have benefited immensely from the knowledge of many great anglers and friends over the years. Mark Antolosky, Skip Galbraith, Charlie Meck, and Walt Young have been more gracious to me than I ever deserved. The days on the water, the hours around the tying bench, and so many evenings at the dinner table are more valuable to me than you know.

I thank my father, Jon P. Stroup (1941–2003) for instilling the desire to cut my own path in whatever venue I chose. He was the greatest man I've ever known and my best friend. His memory will always be an inspiration to me.

Thanks also to my mother, Betty, the ex-English teacher and bow fisherwoman who still can't believe that people pay me to take them fishing and don't get to keep the fish, and to my sisters

Acknowledgments

Megan, Rachael, and Maureen. Your support through the tough times will never be forgotten.

Thanks to the many men and women who have spent a day on the water with me. I have enjoyed every single one of them. To all whom I have had the pleasure of working with over the years. Many thanks.

Special thanks to Sean McGraw. You believed in me at a time when I didn't.

Foreword

Forty years ago I never used a guide. At that time I thought they were an unnecessary part of the fly-fishing fantasy. That all changed when I co-authored *Great Rivers, Great Hatches*. In preparation for that book, I employed 25 different guides on rivers all across the country, and I learned innumerable valuable tactics and techniques from all of them. That experience changed my opinion about guides forever.

Yes, guides are an important aspect of fly fishing, and since my first introduction to professional guides I have employed more than 100. In *Common-Sense Fly Fishing*, Eric Stroup examines fly fishing from the skilled eyes of a guide who is on the water almost half the days of a calendar year and who has watched, coached, and taught thousands of anglers on streams and rivers in Pennsylvania and Montana.

In this book, Stroup incorporates many of the lessons he has learned, both from personal experience and time on the water guiding fellow fly fishers. His seven common-sense principles, along with the illustrations by Dave Hall, take a lot of the guesswork out of what many consider a difficult, and sometimes frustrating, sport. These principles—drift, reading the water, approach, casting, line control, rod position, and mending—simplify fly fishing so that anyone, from beginner to expert, can catch more fish. Eric explains all seven principles in an intricate, clear manner so even the neophyte can readily understand and adopt them. Some of these principles, such as positioning and line control, are critical aspects of fly fishing that few of us seldom consider when we fly fish.

Recognizing and eliminating drag is the one factor that has helped me catch more trout. It is the one aspect of fly fishing that is difficult to convey and plagues beginners and experts. It is the one thing that separates the successful angler from one who experiences constant disappointment. His discussion of drift is invaluable for the beginner and expert. *Common-Sense Fly Fishing* shows you a simplified method of accomplishing a drag-free float, which is so important if you want to consistently catch more trout.

Reading this book is like having a guide accompany you on every trip to a stream, and it should be valuable addition to your fly-fishing library.

Charles Meck
Pennsylvania Furnace, Pennsylvania
September 2009

Introduction

Fly fishing is not rocket science, nor does it need to be. At a very basic level, it is the art of delivering a fly using the current. Any attempt to make it more complicated than that is done so for the pleasure of the angler. One of the appeals of this sport, or recreation (whichever you prefer), is that we can make it as complex and scientific as we want.

Walk into just about any fly shop and listen to all the "experts" talking Latin. I once listened intently to a conversation in my own shop between a couple of locals discussing the trout's preference that day for a gray, rather than a brown, head on a size 28 midge. (For the uninitiated, you can fit about a dozen size 28 midges on your thumbnail.) The conversation then turned into what sounded like Mass, and my attention turned to other things. If I really needed to know what they were biting on, I'd ask my neighbor Skip and he'd tell me, "This little black thing."

Throughout its history, fly fishing has always enjoyed a romantic image. It has been written about for centuries. In more recent times, great American authors have contributed to the volumes of information. Even Hollywood has cashed in on its image.

Fly fishing is bigger than ever, and more people today fish with a fly rod than at any time in history. While participation in the sport is at an all-time high, so is the neverending stream of information on how to do it. As a full-time professional guide, I get to see a lot of anglers fish. Some are good; others are not. Most of what I see looks pretty good to the casual observer, but not to the trout.

The single biggest impediment to anglers' success that I see daily is the lack of what I call fly-fishing common sense. I see hundreds of anglers every season who have a strong command of the mechanics of fly fishing, yet they have no knowledge of what to do with it. This book is designed to help anglers, of all skill levels, achieve success on the trout stream. These are the principles I teach daily, and they will help you deal with most situations you encounter on trout streams across the country.

This book will provide a strong base for any angler to build on that is centered on the single most important factor in fly fishing—the drift. Perhaps only conditions and hungry fish have more value on a trout stream. The best water, equipment, casting, and flies mean absolutely nothing without a good drift. I tell clients that are beginning fly fishers that if they are only able to recognize a good drift by the end of their first day, they will be miles ahead of the curve.

But the concept of a good drift is not limited only to beginners. I once had a client call and book a trip with me. After our initial conversation, I thought that my day with this gentleman (we'll call him Bob) would be a walk in the park. Speaking with him was like talking to Ernie Schwiebert. His knowledge of the local entomology was surprising, and after he dropped a few names of people he had fished with, I couldn't wait to meet him.

During our conversation on the way to the stream, Bob spoke of his adventures the previous week on a spring creek in Montana that I have fished on several occasions and found quite challenging. His success, as he pointed out, was due in large part to his ability to keep an open mind and never be afraid to try something new. Without going into detail here about how he solved the spring creek's mysteries, I'll simply say that when he pulled out a Gary Howe–built Winston bamboo rod, I was sold.

We were fishing a spring creek that has a good population of 14- to 16-inch wild fish. On occasion they can be really spooky, and as I explained this to Bob, he assured me that this was his kind of fishing. He enjoyed the challenge of tough fish, and we shared stories of spending hours (as I have) trying to get a drift to a 9-inch trout in a tough spot.

Blue-Winged Olives were on the water as we approached the stream, and after I finished tying a Harvey slack leader for him, I tied on a size 20 Marinaro-style thorax pattern that my good friend Tom Baltz had tied for me. Tommy is one of the finest fly tiers in the world, and an even better friend. I don't use his flies for guiding . . . ever. This, however, seemed like an appropriate occasion, and my client appreciated it.

We carefully waded into position and found a fat 14-inch brown feeding in a current line that would be easy to get a good drift through. As we prepared to make the first cast, a large fish rose at the top of the run. What was about to unfold I will never forget. Bob began ripping line off of the reel, and with a casting stroke like I've never seen began to hurl fly line in a fashion that can best be described as a Chinese New Year celebration gone wild. The poor rod was stressed at both ends, and all I could think to do was duck.

When the attack was over and it was safe to look up, the little Blue-Winged Olive was buzzing at Mach 4 across the top end of the run. After two more attempts at the large fish there, every fish in the pool was gone. Bob turned to me, looked me right in the eye, and very calmly stated, with the same tone of expertise with which he had solved the Montana spring-creek dilemma, "They don't want that fly."

"Oh, they wanted it, they just couldn't catch it!" I thought.

Bob is at the extreme end of the spectrum when it comes to understanding drift. He had been fishing for years and never fully grasped the concept of delivering flies *with* the current. After reading this book, it should become second nature to you to try to achieve a good drift. It should be your primary focus. Drift determines where you position yourself, how you cast, and how you manage your line.

I hope that *Common-Sense Fly Fishing* will help you be more successful on the stream, and that you in turn will help someone else become better. The future of fly fishing and preservation of our resources depend on anglers like you who appreciate our gifts and the value of a day on the water. Enjoy the book.

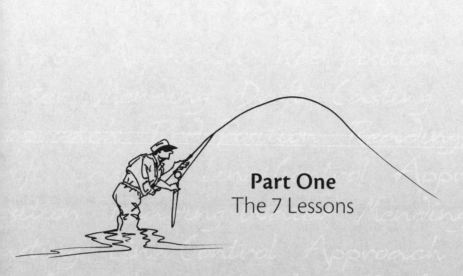

Part One
The 7 Lessons

Chapter 1
Lesson One: Drift

I start this book with a discussion of drift because everything from here on out is based around obtaining a good drift. Everyone has different methods of achieving the same result, and many of these techniques are not unique to me. I have, in my humble opinion, had the pleasure of learning from some of the best anglers in the world, and I'm fortunate to be able to spend nearly every day on some of the best trout water in the East. My clients give me a unique opportunity to see many different techniques and to share proven methods for central Pennsylvania and Montana waters. If there is one thing I have learned over the years—whether you're in Montana, Mongolia, or Pennsylvania—it is that if you want to catch trout consistently, you must be able to achieve a controlled and natural drag-free drift. Understanding what it is and how to obtain it is the first step to better results. A good drift moves at exactly the same speed as the current. A bad drift more often than not is one that will move at an unnaturally fast pace through the current, and it often moves perpendicular to it as well.

As we all know, sometimes an unnatural movement will catch fish. Many times, twitching a fly such as a caddis pattern will entice a trout to take with a vengeance. There is also the deadly time at the end of a drift when your nymph, or nymphs, starts to rise up off the bottom and maybe even swing a little bit. This lift often results in takes so violent, particularly when swinging wet flies, that fish will break off your fly if you are not careful on the set or do not use heavy enough tippet. While imparting motion to flies can be effective, most situations call for a "dead drift."

Achieving a perfect drift, and understanding how to do so, is fundamental to good fly fishing. Poor drifts are the result of the fly being attached to the fly rod, via the fly line and leader, and our inability to adjust and create enough slack to allow the fly to drift naturally. Our goal as anglers is to create this drift and yet still be able to identify a take and set the hook. Drift is the single most important

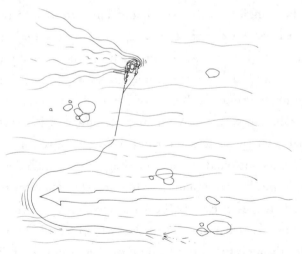

Drag occurs when the current takes all the slack from the line, pulling the fly at an unnaturally fast pace. Drag prevents your nymph from sinking deep and wakes your dry fly across the surface.

aspect of fly fishing. Without an understanding of the concept, and learning how to create a good drift, you won't catch many fish.

Recognize Changing Currents

Rivers and streams follow a course governed by gravity. Within their banks, obstructions, depressions, and bends define the characteristic features of a stream, such as riffles, pools, and runs. These features are made from the causes and effects of millions of speeds of water pushing and pulling their way downstream, all the while creating the beautiful sounds of running water for our listening pleasure. If current speeds were represented by different colors in the spectrum, then nearly every single piece of water we fish would have all the colors of the rainbow from bank to bank. Additionally, surface currents are often faster than the currents on the bottom of the stream, providing an entirely different dimension to consider.

The concept of drift is not just about understanding the current speed that the trout is *in*, it's also about understanding the currents you have to fish *through* to reach the current line that the fish is in. This is what makes fly fishing for trout so interesting and challenging. The environment in which we do this is ever changing. No two days on the trout stream are ever the same. Some streams, depending on their size, can be completely different in only the time span of a month. Consequently, learning a particular piece of water is not enough. You have to learn the basic principles and techniques for achieving a good drift and overcoming drag, so that you are prepared for any situation that you encounter.

For example, from April to June, the Little Juniata River often fishes like three different rivers. One particular run sweeps down-

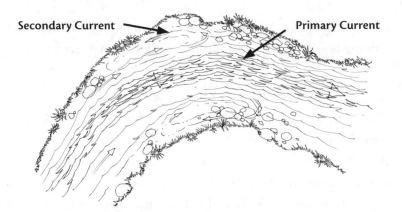

Secondary Current ⟵   Primary Current

In most fishing situations, you will have to contend with many secondary currents each time you present the fly to a fish in the primary current (the current in which the fish is holding or feeding). If possible, move to a position that allows you to reduce the number of secondary currents through which you are fishing.

stream in an S turn from the left to the right. In high water, the middle of this run is a shallow riffle and the bulk of the current is on the edges. In lower water, the current is in the middle of the run. This change in the location of the current has the biggest effect on the run below this riffle. As the water level drops, the main current moves from left to right (looking downstream). This change is barely visible to the casual observer, but the best drift in April is much different than the best drift in May. By June, anglers are fishing the wrong side of the run, standing right where the fish are, because that's where they caught trout earlier in the season.

Understand Primary and Secondary Currents

Bubbles or debris in a current line can help you understand how fast your fly is supposed to be moving by providing a point of

Eliminating drag can be as simple as changing position. Fishing parallel to the current line in which the trout is holding or feeding (right) is often less challenging than fishing perpendicular to the target (left) and across several different current speeds.

reference for the speed of your fly or indicator. But being able to identify and fish through all the secondary currents, many of which you cannot see, that cause drag on your fly is a completely different skill altogether.

Drag occurs when the fly line or leader is lying in or being swept away by a current of a different speed (a secondary current) than that which the fly is in (the primary current). If the secondary current is faster than the primary current that you are fishing, the fly will move faster through the targeted area. If the secondary current is slower, it will swing the fly and pull it toward you. Neither scenario creates a natural drift, and neither catches trout. Your goal is to try and eliminate the effects of all of the secondary currents, which are most often caused or created by the primary current and are usually the defining edges of primary currents. There can be several secondary currents to every primary current in any fishing situation.

The third condition that causes drag is when the leader straightens out completely and immediately pulls the fly. This is why it is critical that you have slack in your leader immediately after you cast. Many anglers think the leader is supposed to straighten out on the cast. This is just flat out wrong. We'll get into leader design later in the book, but it is important to understand that a well-designed leader is what really produces the drag-free drift. You can manage the fly line, but if the leader straightens out from the get-go, achieving a good drift is virtually impossible.

Get As Close As Possible

The first step to creating a good drift is to eliminate as many secondary currents as possible. The best anglers in the world struggle with getting a good drift over multiple secondary currents, so the first rule of thumb is get as close as you can. An old friend and former Pennsylvania Fish Commissioner Rozell (Rozy) Stidd once told me, "We need to teach fishermen to stalk fish, not stock fish." *A River Runs Through It* did no justice to the folks it brought to the sport by showcasing Brad Pitt shadow-casting to a trout 70 feet away, a beautiful but disastrous way to fish. Smart anglers can easily eliminate most situations where long casts are required with a little common sense.

Focus Your Fishing Upstream

Although you can achieve a good drift by fishing downstream, setting the hook and recognizing the take can be extremely difficult. For several reasons, the advantages of fishing upstream far outweigh any downstream advantages. First, since trout face into the current, and most currents travel downstream (eddies are one notable exception), you can typically get closer to a trout when you approach it from behind, or downstream. Additionally, you are able to eliminate most, if not all, of the secondary currents because

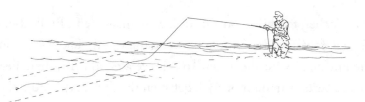

A proactive approach to controlled slack and mending allows you to keep the slack you need between the rod tip and the fly, and not where the stream's currents push it. Fishing upstream helps you maintain proper rod position through the drift.

you are fishing parallel to the target rather than across stream, or perpendicular, to it.

Also, when nymphing you can control the depth of your flies with the distance you cast ahead of the trout. Casting from below the trout requires minimal mending to sink your fly. When positioned downstream, there is very little tension on the line. You are doing little more than collecting slack and everything is moving in the same general direction, allowing the flies to sink through the entire drift and stay deep. If you are above the flies, the slightest mend will either prevent the flies from getting deep or, worse, actually pull the flies up through the current. Even though this is momentary, and may be nothing more than a split second of time, it is time that the flies are not sinking. This is caused by surface tension on the fly line and hard to avoid unless the drift is executed perfectly. The mend will actually stop the drift of the flies, which, in moving water, prevents them from reaching bottom.

Control Your Slack

Any time the fly or indicator is upstream of the rod tip, and the fly line is somewhere in between the two, you can achieve a good drift. When teaching controlled slack management, I talk about a 3- to 4-foot corridor created between the rod tip and the fly once the line and fly hit the water. To achieve a good drift, there needs to be a certain amount of slack between the fly and the rod tip, but it must be contained within this space.

Though a good starting point for the corridor's width is 3 to 4 feet, that really depends on your ability to manage slack. You must not have so much line on the water that you can't set the hook. Distance exacerbates the problem because of the sheer amount of line on the water. If you are fishing a dry fly 30 or more feet away, the corridor needs to be narrow to increase your chances of a good hook-set.

Another facet of controlling slack is that it does no good to set the slack aside in another current after you mend. Many anglers react to a poor cast or bad position by simply moving poorly positioned line to another bad position in order to buy time for the drift. This book will teach you to proactively beat drag through positioning, casting, and the proper use of line control.

Chapter 2
Lesson Two: Reading Water

Learning how to find fish is an essential skill for successful fly fishing, and the best place to start is by understanding your quarry. Trout live in many different types of water, ranging from cold, placid lakes to large rivers to small mountain brooks. In most stillwater situations, such as lakes, ponds, and slow pools, trout often search for their food, and great fun can be had sight-fishing for cruisers. However, the skill of reading water is paramount in moving streams and rivers where the trout are abundant but not often seen. Reading water, like reading a map, is a way of determining the most likely places in a stream that will hold trout.

Food and Safety

Trout are supreme economists. In streams and rivers where trout live in an unending flow of current, survival depends greatly on the fishes' ability to use less energy than they take in. This is extremely important information for fly fishers, who, for the most part, use the current to deliver their flies to fish. Even with active streamer-

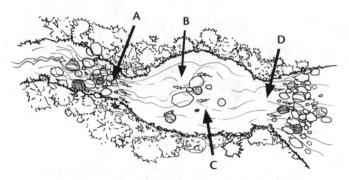

Being able to read the water will help you fish more effectively. (A) and (D) are good feeding lies, and if there was a nice drop-off at the head of the pool, (A) would be a prime lie. Rocks in the deep part of the pool provide typical sheltering lies (C), and fish holding in front of rocks are often in prime lies (B).

fishing retrieves it is essential to understand both the location of the trout and how the currents are moving.

Safety is a primary concern for trout. By the time they are adults, they have few enemies in the water, but lots of threats from above. Predators such as eagles, herons, hawks, mink, and humans condition them to spend their lives in concealment, and they are extremely wary—the shadow of a robin flying over the water can send a fish to cover. For this reason, it is important that you avoid being seen by your quarry.

Sheltering lies are places in the stream that offer trout safety. Because the depth of deep runs and pools offer trout some of the best protection, they hold fish year-round. And, these areas are also some of the most targeted by anglers. Because of the fishing pressure, I generally pass these pools by, instead focusing on other, more productive, areas of a trout stream. I do fish deep pools and runs during the off-season when water temperatures are at their coldest and I know the fish will be stacked in them. Fish will often take refuge in these areas during the hot summer months as well, but catching them and pulling them through the warm surface water can stress them too much.

Feeding lies are places that may not offer all the safety of sheltering lies but have enough current and deliver enough food that the reward outweighs the risk. Feeding lies may be best described as areas that trout inhabit only during times when there is food available to them, such as shallow riffles, backeddies, or pool tailouts where trout migrate during a heavy hatch or spinner fall. These lies are most often inhabited during periods of low light or good hatches. Most of the time, I prefer to target trout that are feeding. Not only are they more willing to take your fly, but they are not hunkered down tight to structure or in really deep water, which makes them easier to catch.

Prime lies offer both food and safety and always hold fish. Generally, the biggest or most dominate fish will hold in the best lies, which are the prime lies. A prime lie typically will have a good source of current that delivers food and oxygen and also have structure or depth (or both) to provide safety. These lies do not need to be the deepest holes in the river, and I have often come across them by luck. One that I've discovered on my home water is a depression on the leading edge of a rock in less than two feet of water. It holds big fish every year, and I'm sure many anglers walk past it—as I did for a long time. Similar rocks surrounding it don't hold fish, but this particular one always does.

Bubble lines are another clue to use in finding trout and are a good indicator of feeding lanes. They are the result of where multiple currents converge and funnel debris, foam, and food downstream. Watch a bubble line during a spinner fall and you'll

When currents collide, foam, bubbles, debris, and food are funneled into distinct lines that often indicate current edges that are otherwise invisible. Trout feed here, often right on the edges, so that they don't have to fight the continuous current. Foam is home.

undoubtedly see heads sipping right in the foam. A good foam line will also define edges of current that might be very difficult to see otherwise.

Water Level, Temperature, and Clarity

Water level and depth play an important role in where fish hold. Early in the season, when levels are up on freestone rivers, fish will rest and feed in different areas than in summer's low flows. This was never more evident than one recent season on my home water. During the spring, the river was full of water. The level was right at the top end of where I consider it fishable, but due to our busy guiding schedule we fished it regardless.

There's an old saying that goes "I'd rather be lucky than good," and I must say I got very lucky. While guiding during the early season, I happened to hit a piece of water that I don't normally fish very hard, for no other reason than I've never done particularly well there. It's not bad looking water, but few people ever fish it for I'm sure the same reason. But because of this season's abnormally high water, this water was holding fish—a lot of fish. We had several 50-fish days, and it wasn't just one run, it was any run on the river that had roughly three to four feet of depth and moderate current velocity.

Higher water had transformed what were typically feeding lies into prime lies. During our heaviest hatches, which usually produce stellar dry-fly fishing, the fish never rose consistently because they were all stacked in this type of water. I heard other fishermen complaining that the hatch was terrible and the fish weren't on the bugs, but the truth was the fish were eating nymphs all day long in these deep, slow runs. It was some of the best fishing I've ever witnessed; it just wasn't on the surface insects. So the lesson here is that depth of water will have a lot to do with where the trout are going to be. Always ask yourself, "Where are the trout going to be the safest and get the most food by using the least amount of energy?" That is where you want to begin.

Clarity of water is the next consideration when it comes to looking for trout. Clear water makes our job as anglers more difficult, so in these conditions, you should concentrate on depth and broken water. Depth can be anything from a green-colored run to the back side of a rock that's been chewed out by the current. Safety will be first and foremost in the trout's mind when the water is clear. If you do see a fish out in the open, be assured that it feels safe enough to be there because it can see its surroundings well. On sunny days, fishing clear water can be frustrating to say the least, so look to the broken water. Any water that has a broken surface can produce good results. I have found trout in less than half a foot of water in these conditions.

Temperature is another important part of finding fish. If you're in an area where summer water temperatures reach 70 degrees, carry a thermometer. I always recommend that anglers don't fish when temperatures rise to these levels, but many Eastern freestone streams with huge spring influences can fish fine once you find the springs. If you are fishing in a stream that has a lot of springs, a thermometer will help you find the cooler areas, as well as stay away from the areas where the water is too warm.

Again, as temperatures begin to creep up over 68 degrees, trout will be looking for oxygenated water. As temperatures warm, oxygen molecules expand. Trout have a small amount of gill surface and cannot absorb the larger oxygen molecules the way that bass, with a large gill surface, can. Consequently, trout need to find areas where the water tumbles and the molecules are broken into smaller units that they can absorb. So what you're looking for is literally broken water.

Structure

I caught my first trout from behind a rock, and then I spent the next ten years looking for rocks, as well as other structure such as stumps, rocks, tires, and even old refrigerators. Though I have since learned that trout can be found in many other areas of the stream, structure is always a great place to start. All fish like structure. In addition to safety, structure can also provide better feeding opportunities and even relief from the light and heat of the sun. However, to fish structure well, you have to understand how the current works around it.

Every piece of structure is different. Notice where the depth is. Is the depth in front or behind the structure? If the front (up-

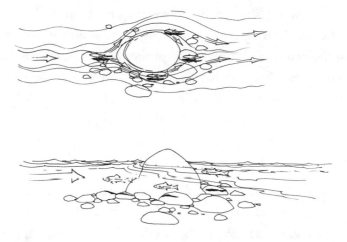

Any structure can create multiple lies. Current speed and depth are critical. If the current is moderate and wraps around the rock, there is often a feeding lie behind the rock (above). In faster water, this spot might only be a sheltering lie.

stream) of the structure is deep, that is more than likely going to be the prime lie. If the downstream side is deep as well, there are two major lies on either side where a fish can stay out of the current, yet still pick off food coming around the structure in the current. Often, you'll find the current on one side of the structure to be stronger than on the other, and I have often found the prime lie to be on the side with the weaker current. My guess is that there is roughly the same amount of food being split between either side of the structure and less current to fight on the weaker side.

Structure is not limited to objects in the current line. Structure can also be a fallen tree on the edge of the stream or even an overhanging branch that provides a trout protection from above, or better yet, a perch from which ants and beetles fall into the stream during summer. Low overhanging branches can be fantastic areas during heavy caddis flights as often the bugs will rest on the branches and fall to the surface during heavy wind or rain. During the Grannom hatch in central Pennsylvania, we will often find trout holding right below overhanging limbs, ready to take any unlucky insects that fall off the branches.

Depth

Reading the water is not all that difficult with the understanding that current delivers the food, and depth equals safety. Depth plus current equals trout. Here in the East, many of our limestone streams have a bit of color to them throughout the year, and often two feet of water will hide a fish. I often tell beginners to stay away from areas where they can see the bottom clearly. In many freestone streams, trout will hold in deep water where the bottom is clearly visible, so approach the stream stealthily and as though you're hunting.

There is a fine line between getting close enough to simplify your presentation and staying far enough away from trout (especially wild fish) so that you do not spook them. The closer you are the less line you have to manage, the easier it is to cast accurately, and the better chances you have of getting a good drift. But, the fish can't know that you are there. How close you can get depends on the lighting conditions, water clarity, and how heavily the fish are feeding (among other things), so it is best to err on the side of caution and slowly work your way closer to the fish until you can get a feel for how close you can get.

Chapter 3
Lesson Three: Approach

Dead-drifting a fly to a trout is a completely visual game. It is very rare to actually feel the take, though it does sometimes happen. Takes are a matter of the trout simply opening their mouths and accepting the fly, acts so subtle that we probably don't see half of them. Because of this, we have to make the most of what little advantage we can gain through proper positioning. Ultimately, your ability to identify and get into the best position will account for far more successes than any fly pattern or expensive rod.

Your position in the stream can make or break a good drift. It can be extremely difficult to achieve a drift over multiple secondary currents, and it is even more difficult to achieve the desired depth if you're nymphing. Proper positioning in the stream not only improves your presentation, it sets you up for proper line control. With the correct position, you can almost always eliminate at least one secondary current, and in some cases eliminate secondary currents altogether.

Identify a Target

A quarterback doesn't just throw the ball down the field, hoping that someone will catch it. Acquire a target, and a game plan, by reading the water or spotting a feeding fish. Then, get in a good position to catch it.

Your first consideration when thinking about the best position is drift. How close can you get? Where do you need to be to achieve a drift, and how many secondary currents are you dealing with? I start close. My first thought is always, "Can I high-stick this with no line on the water?" Sometimes it's not physically possible to get this close to the fish; other times, it's not practical—you will either spook the fish or the water is too deep to wade any closer.

My goal is to get close enough that I only have one secondary current to deal with. If I can achieve that, I can most likely make a cast so that my line is in a position where I will be able to manage it and mend it in time to get the drift. If I'm not able to get that close to the target, I will try to position myself where I have two secondary currents, and I'll eliminate the effects of one of them with my line positioning in the cast, which I'll discuss in the next chapter.

Let's run through the best approaches for a few common situations.

Fishing Rocks

The stream is approximately 50 feet across and has an average depth of two feet. The water is low and clear, and in the center of the stream a large boulder protrudes from the water, splitting the current. The deepest part of the structure is at the head (upstream) of the boulder, and both sides of the boulder are surrounded by

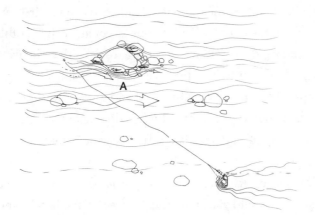

This position (approximately 8 o'clock) will require the least amount of mending, will not spook the fish, and will allow the flies to naturally drift right into the structure. Note that the fly line may be at an angle to the rock, but it is parallel to the current deflected off the rock (A).

dark, emerald-green water. The pocket behind the boulder is filled in with light-colored sand and doesn't have much depth. The current is of moderate speed, and aside from the current around the structure, the water is like glass, with the bottom of the stream visible. You've not seen a rise, though it is June and there are plenty of caddis in the air, so you are wisely fishing a generic Elk-Hair Caddis with a beadhead nymph on a two-foot dropper.

You'll never be able to get close to the rock because the water is too low and clear. Because you will have to stay back, you need to decide where to position yourself in relation to the rock to get the best drift. If the boulder is the center of the clock, straight upstream is 12 o'clock. You are on the left side of the river looking upstream, which is roughly at the 9 o'clock position.

First, examine an approach from 6 o'clock, directly downstream from the boulder. To hit your target at the head of the rock, you would need to cast far beyond the rock so that the fly drifts to the fish. This is problematic because the current forming around the edge of the rock is slightly faster than the current where the fly lands. When the current, which is flowing at an even pace, hits the rock, it splits and speeds up. It zips around the rock like water draining out of a tub moves when it finally gets close enough to the drain when it speeds up, spins around, and disappears. This acceleration would occur in the fly line immediately and begin speeding up the fly prematurely, so your fly will drag through the target area and your nymph will not get deep enough to reach the fish. Not only will this not catch fish, it may very well spook them.

From the 8 o'clock position, you can cast parallel to the current deflected off of the rock. This should allow you to cast far enough ahead of the rock to achieve the right depth with the nymph, and should also provide a nice presentation along the edge of the rock. This position also gives you a good angle on the hook-set. Additionally, from here you are still downstream of the boulder and can move and fish the other side of the rock without much disturbance after you've fished the near side.

The 9 to 12 o'clock positions could work as well with the right type of cast, depending on the water clarity. These positions can make the hook-set difficult, as they would require more slack to get the drift. The 9 o'clock position would require less line but a good mend since you would be casting almost perpendicular to the current.

The key in this situation is to identify the direction of the current that you want to drift your fly to, and cast so that your line and fly land in a corridor in line with that current. Common sense tells us to always start below the trout. There are very few times where this approach will be wrong. If the current is flowing toward you, you have an advantage to overcoming its detrimental effects. When you are above the current, you are forced to feed additional line into the drift to achieve the same effects. The point at which you lose the advantage is when the flies are below you and you lose the amount of slack, the manipulation of line, and the hooking angle advantages. That's not to say you can't or won't catch a trout this way, you just lose your advantage.

Example 2: Bend Run

Facing downstream, the river takes a hard right turn and forges a deep run right through its center. This is a perfect run to nymph, yet it poses some challenges. Whenever the inside edge of a turn is dead water with little or no movement, as this one is, in almost all cases the best position from which to fish is the inside of the bend. Depending on the size of the river, you'll either want to be on the inside of the bend, or, in the case of a smaller stream, at the bottom end of the run and cast up into it. In either case, the flies will have to land in the uppermost part of the run and flow through the bend to get deep enough by the time they reach the best holding water.

The tricky part to this scenario is that from either position part of the fly line is going to be in the slack water on the inside of the bend, while the business end of your tackle (the end of the fly line, the leader, and flies) is going to be moving rapidly through the heavier, faster current. You are going to have to mend the fly line in the slack water downstream (if you are on the inside of the bend) or to the right, into the current (if you were at the bottom of the run). The correct positioning is where you are most likely able to succeed at making the correct mends and achieve the drift.

A small section of stream that I fish with clients has this exact scenario. It's a deep run that always holds a lot of fish, and we've fished it both from the inside of the bend and from the bottom of the run. Over the years, I have learned that the correct position is in the middle of the bend. This is where you have complete control of the drift and fly line throughout the entire drift and never need any more line or slack than is absolutely necessary. To drift the entire bend, you need to make four to five relatively easy mends that, because of your position, never line the fish. If you try to present the fly from the bottom of the run, you must throw a long mend into the current that is holding the fish, which often spooks them.

Have a Plan

All too often, I see anglers charge right up to the head of the pool and begin fishing, which is not always the most efficient or effective way of covering the water. When guiding, I like to approach a particular piece of water with my client and explain in detail how we plan to fish it. This conversation is almost always at the tail end of the water, and I point out the different current lines and edges before we start. I might say something such as "We're going to pay particular attention to the inside seam and work that really hard before we move on." I try to give the client a plan to fish the water effectively.

When you're evaluating how to fish a section of water, create a map in your mind so that you can cover it all. When I'm guiding,

I have to take advantage of the available water. We fish mostly on public water, and that means that we are often fishing in and amongst other anglers. When we do have the luxury of a piece of water to ourselves, we do not squander it and fish it all. Now there is something to be said for solitude, and when few anglers are on the water, especially in the off season, I will often jump to the best areas and lies and skip over the less productive pieces of water. However, when I take a client to a particular stretch, I make a plan to cover it all. This often means fishing water that I know might be less productive in certain places. But guess what? We regularly catch fish out of those places. Other anglers walk right past a lot of that water, so it doesn't get near the pressure that every good looking run gets.

Some of the best trout fishermen I know do not walk past much. They fish it all and catch fish out of all of it. Sometimes I find that the reason I think poorly of an area of stream has more to do with its difficulty to fish, rather than its population of fish. Good trout rivers and streams have trout everywhere, not just where we catch them. You'll be well-served to fish all the water, and may just surprise yourself with how well you do in areas you normally walk right by.

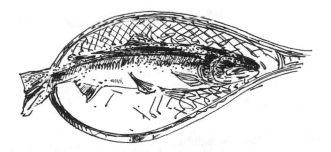

Chapter 4
Lesson Four: Casting

Anyone who tells you that you don't have to be a good caster to be a good fly fisherman is one of two things. Either they are not a good caster, or they're not a good fly fisherman. The best fishermen I know are all excellent casters, and quite frankly, it is their ability to cast that makes them so good. Saying you don't need to be able to cast well in fly fishing is like saying you don't need to be able to run to play in the NFL. The cast is what delivers the goods, and a good cast sets everything else up properly.

Being able to throw 90 feet of line means nothing and has no purpose in trout fishing. Though we all like to see how much line we can get out when we're in the yard, it is no measure of fishing ability. Distance certainly has advantages, especially during those times of year when conditions make getting close tough. But in most cases on a trout stream the ability to bring the fly either inside or outside of the stroke, the ability to lay the line upstream or downstream of the fly, and the ability to place a fly in a cup at 30 feet is what counts. You show me someone who can make a tuck cast, a slack-leader cast, and a 30-foot roll cast, and I'll show you a good fisherman.

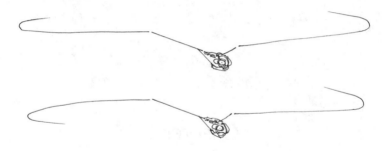

Being able to bring the fly on both the inside and outside of the casting stroke allows you to place your fly line in the proper position with the cast, eliminating the need to make a reactionary mend.

As a guide, I get to see a lot of different casting strokes. Some of the most unorthodox strokes work and some of the prettiest, picture-perfect strokes don't. Unfortunately, time limitations of a guided day often prevent holding a casting clinic, so guides try to put a band-aid on the problems and try to get the client into fish. I do see, however, over the course of many years, some common tendencies that I will try to address here. There is no substitute for practice, and while I am going to cover techniques and procedures that have worked for me, these are by no means the only way to accomplish the goal. You can compare a casting stroke to a golf swing. The principles that make both work are similar, but no two golfers in the PGA have the same stroke, and no two fly casters will either. Try to understand the concept, and then put it to use in your own way.

Tuck Cast

The tuck cast was developed by the late George Harvey as a means of getting nymphs deep quickly. Joe Humphreys, Harvey's

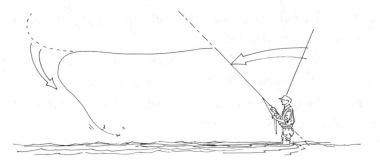

In the tuck cast (above), the abrupt stop on the forward stroke drives the flies into the water before the leader or line. This gets them to the bottom quickly, and the absence of fly line or leader on the water helps create a drag-free drift.

protégé, has perfected this cast and has taught it for the past 50 years. The tuck cast is used primarily with nymphing rigs, though I often use it with dry/dropper rigs as well. The cast requires a lot of power on the forward stroke and a high, abrupt stop at the end that drives the weighted rig into the water, forcing the flies and weight to the bottom.

The key to this cast is that the flies touch the water before anything else. Because there is nothing else on the surface to create tension, the flies sink immediately. This makes the rig fishable right from the delivery, and a good fisherman will employ good line handling skills and have control of the rig and the slack through the entire drift.

In teaching the tuck cast over the years, I have learned a few tips that make this cast easier. First, the cast has to be performed in two different planes. You should make the back cast at the three-quarters side-arm position, and the forward cast should be vertical. This eliminates the chance of running the nymphs and split-shot into the rod tip.

The second tip is to throw the back cast high. The normal ten to two stroke should be tightened slightly, and the stroke should be more like ten and one. The stroke employs more acceleration in both the back and forward stroke, and you must let the rod load before coming forward. The only way to cause the flies to tuck under is to build so much momentum coming forward that the flies are driven down into the water when the line is stopped on the forward stroke. As the flies are driven down, the fly line jumps up in the opposite direction, giving you an opportunity to either keep it off the water entirely or mend. Extreme discipline is required at the delivery to stop the rod and allow the terminal end of your tackle to do what it's supposed to do.

Slack-Leader Cast

During the summer of 2009, I was on the Stillwater River in Nye, Montana, with Joe Humphreys running a clinic for the USA Youth Fly Fishing Team. As the kids finished my clinic on controlled slack, they would then wade a hundred yards upstream to Humphreys' clinic on streamer techniques. In between sessions, in the midst of a tremendous storm that was brewing to the west, Joe began to work his way downstream, fishing the far edge of the river with a hopper. He was throwing 60 feet of line and laying the hopper four inches from the bank with pinpoint accuracy. The more amazing fact was that he was getting a perfect drift for at least 6 to 8 seconds.

The Stillwater River is a wide river with good flow through most of its width, but the edges (where the trout are so often) are

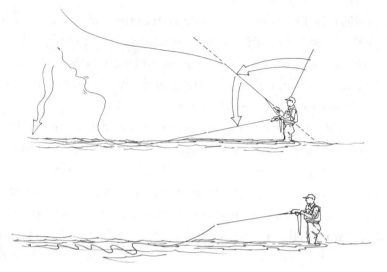

To make a good slack-leader cast, you must come forward with high line speed and stop abruptly so that the leader recoils and falls on the water in a series of S curves. If done properly, the fly will land on the water at almost the same time as the end of the fly line.

almost void of any current. I watched Joe cover every inch of the shoreline with that hopper until he had made his way down to where Lance Wilt (one of our guides) and I were standing. Joe then called us out into the water and gave us a brief lesson in the way that George Harvey used to teach the cast that he had just used to dissect the banks of the Stillwater.

The slack-leader cast is designed to do exactly what the name implies, put slack in the leader to give the fly a perfectly natural drift. I've seen many try make this cast, and I rarely see anyone do it the right way. Most attempts that I see place slack in the fly line, not the leader. Consequently, when the attempt is made to mend or collect the line, the slack is pulled out of the leader (if there was any there to begin with). One important element to this is obviously the leader, which we will discuss at length later in the text. For now, however, we'll concentrate on the mechanics of the cast and discuss its application on the stream.

The slack-leader cast is an effective way of delivering dry flies with a perfect, natural drift. Begin your forward stroke toward your target, and aim your cast high, depending on the amount of slack that you need—10, 15, even 20 feet above the water's surface. You must have enough line speed on the forward cast, and an abrupt stop, so that the fly and leader recoil back toward you when the line is fully extended at the end of the cast. Like the tuck cast, this is a high speed cast with a lot of velocity. The purpose of the velocity is to both cause the shock and minimize chances of the wind blowing the cast off course. A slow delivery of this cast can also result in the current pulling on the fly line by the time the fly lands, thus minimizing the purpose of the cast.

To prevent tangles I move the rod tip in a circular path, keeping the fly outside of my forward stroke. The forward stroke should end with the reel at or above eye level and the casting arm fully extended. The casting arm and the rod should form a perfectly straight line and be pitched at a 45-degree angle. After the abrupt stop, drop your arm and the rod to waist level. Then drop the rod tip to the water's surface so that the tension of the water surface on the fly line stops the forward progress of the cast. The leader, if the cast is executed properly, will fall on itself in a series of S curves. There will be some slack built into the fly line, but the majority of the slack produced with this technique will be generated in the leader. At this point, pick the rod back up into a fishing position.

The Grip

I always tell my clients to let the rod do the work and that starts with the grip. Every graphite rod has a spline, which is where the graphite sheet, which was once flat, is connected to the other edge after it was rolled. This is a part of the graphite that has a greater diameter than the rest of the rod and is the strength of the rod. The spline is located either on the top of the rod or on the bottom where the guides are, depending on the builder.

There is some debate among builders on whether the strength of the rod should be used for fish fighting or casting, and many builders I know will consider the weight and purpose of the rod in their decision process of where to place the spline. But, the spline is either directly over the guides, or directly under the guides. If you research rod building techniques, every manufacturer and builder will caution against placing the guides on the sides of the blank.

The reasoning is that the graphite is weakest here and the resins and fibers that make the graphite strong will eventually

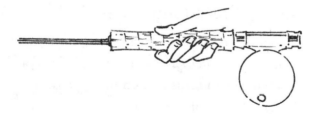

The grip on a fly rod is as important as the grip on a golf club or tennis racquet. I recommend a thumb-on-top grip that is firm, but not tight. Keep your hand far enough up the cork to allow room between the pinky finger and the reel so that you can easily strip line from the reel.

weaken and separate, and the rod will cast like a lazy dog. So what does that tell us about our grip? It tells me that it is much more important than we usually give it credit for. If the fly rod is designed to have a strong side, then our grip should use the design of the rod. The thumb should be placed directly on the cork, opposite the reel. The reel, thumb, and tip of the rod should all be in alignment, all the time. If you have a tendency to turn your wrist when casting, you're not using the strength of the rod and thus are wasting power.

An open wrist in the casting stroke is certainly not catastrophic, but can be problematic. It's not necessarily because the wrist is opened up during the cast, but more because it causes the angler to "slice" the casting stroke. An open wrist will often lead to other problems. Less wrist movement in general is better with regard to casting and a proper grip will often keep unwanted wrist movement to a minimum. The wrist should finish the casting stroke, both in the forward and back cast. It should not be the source of power for the cast. A proper grip makes this possible.

Curing Creep (and Other Tips)

Instructors typically define the casting stroke as occurring between 10 and 2 o'clock. This is a good place to begin, and if you can keep your movements confined to this area on the hypothetical clock, you will generally be better off. Too much movement within the stroke is a common problem, and having a well-defined starting and ending point is a step in the right direction. What's most important, however, is what happens within those points.

I once heard Dan Bailey give an excellent presentation in which he likened casting a fly rod to throwing a potato off the end

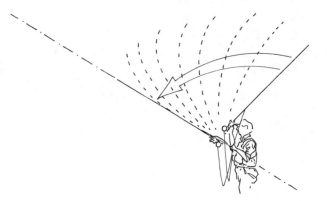

In a smooth, efficient casting stroke, both the forward and back cast require an acceleration to a stop. The illustration shows the application of power through the forward cast by the flex in the moving rod. The same acceleration is applied to the back cast just before the stop.

of a hoe. The casting stroke is an acceleration to a stop. In other words, from the moment you begin to move the rod, it accelerates until it stops. I liken it to a golf stroke. The golf stroke is accelerated all the way through to impact with the ball, much like the casting stroke is accelerated through the loop. In golf, there is a follow through, whereas in fly casting there is a stop, but too much power too early will ruin both kinds of strokes.

The most powerful part of the casting stroke should occur just before the stop. When I teach casting, I teach my students to apply equal power to the back and the forward casts. On the stream, this doesn't always apply, as there are many instances and casts that require different power strokes; however, it is important to understand the amount of power that is necessary to load the rod, and that you apply enough power to execute the stop properly.

When an angler pulls the fly line out of the water to execute a back cast, the rod movement should begin slow and accelerate to

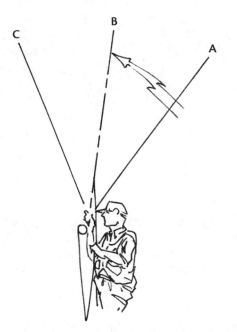

Creep occurs when you stop on your back cast **(A)** *and then slowly creep the rod forward* **(B)** *before beginning the forward stroke. This not only robs the cast of efficiency because the distance from* **(B)** *to* **(C)** *is almost half that of* **(A)** *to* **(C)**, *but it is also causes tailing loops and other presentation problems.*

the point where it stops. As the line is moving back, it will begin to slow down. As this occurs, you can then begin bringing the rod forward. Again, this should begin slow and accelerate to the stop. When the change of direction occurs too rapidly, or begins with too much power (without acceleration), a tailing loop occurs or the fly lands right next to the end of the fly line. Casting is timing and pace, not power. It is important to use enough power to create the energy needed, and once the energy begins to dissipate in one direction, you must apply energy in the other direction.

The stop is extremely critical to the casting stroke, and you must begin your forward cast where you stopped. Many anglers stop at 2 o'clock and then slowly creep the rod forward to 12 o'clock before beginning to execute the forward part of the stroke. Once the rod reaches vertical (12 o'clock), the only way to generate enough power to execute the forward stroke is to start it too quickly, usually with the wrist. The result is either a tailing loop or a cast where the fly lands right next to the end of the fly line. The forward cast is severely underpowered and no matter how much strength you put into it, you can't get the fly to the fish.

To help cure this problem, Joan Wulff instructs her students to stop the rod, and then drift back four inches before beginning the forward stroke. This helps some of my clients, but occasionally it translates into a choppy, tangled mess. If you have a problem with rod creep and have difficulty correcting it, try the following exercise. Between 10 and 2 o'clock, move the rod tip in the shape of an oval, without ever stopping it completely. Make a back cast as you normally would, accelerating to the point where you would normally stop, bringing the fly and the fly line around the outside of the stroke. Then, move the rod tip in a clockwise motion to a point that is more vertical above your head, and begin the forward stroke. As you get comfortable with this, tighten up the stroke to the confines of 11 and 1 o'clock and you will tighten your loop.

If the rod is loaded, it doesn't matter how you bring it forward, the line and fly will travel over the rod tip toward the intended direction. The act of moving the tip in a clockwise motion is simply buying time and keeping the rod in a loaded position. Once this occurs, the rod can come forward in any position. This position can be vertical, and bring the fly directly over the tip, or it can be three-quarters sidearm and bring the fly to the outside of the tip.

One method of fixing creep is to slightly round off the casting stroke. Instead of casting in the same plane (front and back), move the rod tip in an oval. This slight motion, which is accentuated in the illustration, not only loads the rod and encourages a smoother, continuous stroke, it also prevents tangles.

Or, it could come three quarters the other way and bring the fly through the inside of the cast.

I regularly have my clients perform a false-casting exercise with the rod in a vertical position, where I have them bring the fly forward on either side of the stroke. This simple manipulation of rod angle on the forward stroke has tremendous advantages. The ability to get the fly where it needs to be is half of the game. The other half is placing the line in the right position. This is what separates good casters from average. A good caster will get better drifts with less mending, and ultimately catch more fish.

Chapter 5
Lesson Five: Line Control

L et's say I have the most beautiful car on the planet, though anyone who's ever booked a day with me knows better. Hypothetically speaking, I have a beautiful car. This vehicle has plush leather and air conditioning, goes 0 to 60 mph in no time, handles like an absolute dream, and gets great gas mileage. There's only one catch: It has no brakes. Would you drive it? Of course not.

The index finger on your rod hand is just as important to the fly rod as the brakes are on your car. It is in a consistent place and is the only thing near the rod that can tighten the line at any moment. It allows you to keep the perfect amount of line out of the end of the rod as is necessary, and, in conjunction with your other hand, can do the work on 90 percent of the trout you catch.

All the fly-fishing skills in the world are for naught without command of the line. Line control is the single most important, yet forgotten, discipline in the sport, and it is the most frustrating for a guide to deal with. It's simple, but it is also the toughest to teach. Why? Because old habits die hard, and there is very little time or energy dedicated to it in our schools, literature, and practice. We place such a heavy emphasis on our presentation skills that one might think that once we raise a trout, the game is over. But, in reality, the game has just begun.

Several years ago, I was on the Kootenai River in northwest Montana with an old client, who we'll call Tommy. (Sorry Tommy, had to use your real name on this one.) We were drifting right below the dam in an area known for big rainbows, and Tommy was in the front of the boat. Now, I'll be sensitive as to how I'll say this, but despite years of instruction, Tommy has never achieved any semblance of what one would call line control.

Tommy is a line biter. Once he sets the hook he frantically, like a great white shark, starts to search for the line with his face, choppers going full speed, looking for anything to bite onto. Once contact is made, the choppers hold onto the line until Tommy can reach for, and pull, some more line. And when he does, he uses his face to keep biting more line. Despite my best efforts over the years, I've never been able to correct it. Old habits die hard.

On this day, Tommy hit a beautiful 18-inch wild rainbow and went right to work. He attacked the line like a doberman, and while he had a good grip with his teeth, the 'bow jumped right at the boat, sending fly line around Tommy's head. A knot formed around the flip-focals perched on his hat, but there was no time untangle it. The 'bow was running downstream, and all Tommy could do was grit his teeth and hang on. Tommy could not see well

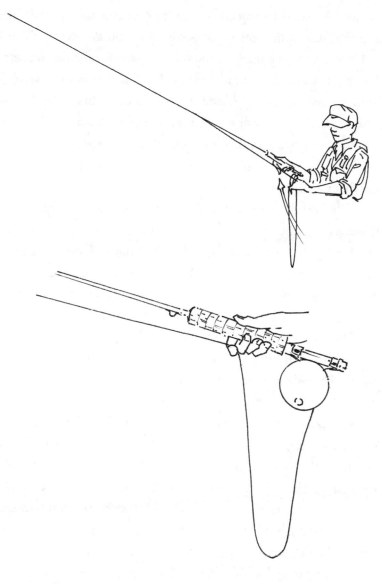

One of the key ingredients to line control is getting the line under your rod hand finger immediately after the cast. Take your line hand to the rod hand. Don't try to reach the line with your rod hand.

because of the line wrapped around his head, the back of the chair, and the back of the reel, so all our guide could do was row as fast as he could to keep up with the fish. A quarter-mile downstream, I jumped out of the boat and netted the fish that tried to strangle Tommy, and we got a picture. I never knew fishing could be so dangerous. A larger fish could have decapitated him. If that's not reason to practice good line control, I don't know what is.

Line control is really simple. It begins and ends with placing the fly line underneath your index finger on your rod hand. That's it, really. While casting, the line runs through the non-casting hand. When the cast is delivered, grasp the line with the non-casting hand and transfer it under the finger of your rod hand. Strip out the excess line from behind the index finger with the non-casting hand. Continue to leave the line under the index finger of your rod hand, and strip from behind that finger.

Once the cast is delivered, the rod should not be moved unless it's used to mend the line or set the hook. The non-casting hand should be gathering line and taking it to the rod hand. When I make a cast, I usually keep a few feet of additional fly line off the reel so I can easily reach up and grab it to begin to strip. I also use that extra line if I need to mend after the cast. Many anglers that I watch will make a great cast, and while trying to get control of the line, they start to reach with the rod hand for the line in their non-casting hand. By doing so, they've moved the rod so much that they've taken all the slack out of the leader, moved the fly, and ruined their chances for a good drift. By the time they gain control of the line, the fly has floated past the target, and they are ready to pick up to make the next cast.

Line control is also important in casting, especially during the pickup. Anglers tend to carry too much line in the air, and regardless of how well you cast, this makes accuracy difficult. This problem usually begins with the pickup. Every angler has a distance that he can carry in the air well. I know for myself that once I surpass that distance, I look and cast like I've never had a rod in my hands before. There is no rule that says you have to cast the same amount of line you're fishing. Carry less line in the air and shoot line for extra distance, if required. This may mean stripping in 10 or 12 feet before making the next cast, but you'll generally make fewer casting mistakes if you do.

Fighting fish exposes poor line control technique quickly and mistakes have a long lasting sting, especially when large trout are lost. I see more trout lost every season when the angler is trying to get the fish on the reel. Who came up with this idea? This is not a requirement once you hook the fish. In fact, most guys who take the time to put fish on the reel still grab the line anyway while they're fighting the fish. Don't waste your time. A big trout will take all your line, and you'll end up on the reel whether you want to be or not, so don't worry about it. You can apply perfect pressure with your finger on the line, and if the fish starts to run on you, keep the pressure on the line and let it take some. The most important part of fighting a fish this way is to remember to strip line behind your finger, not in front. The index finger is the brake. Use it that way. You'll never lose a fish because you let up on the pressure, and trust me you can strip a lot faster than you can reel.

Line Control Tips

Line control begins the minute you step in the water. If your flies aren't in the water drifting over trout, you're not going to catch very many. All too often, I see anglers fussing around with their line, trying to get it out of the guides, trying to get enough line out to cast, trying to get the line unwrapped from their rod, reel, and themselves. This is wasting valuable fishing time, and it is also frustrating. Here are a few simple tips to help.

DOUBLE IT OVER

When you begin your day and you're stringing up your fly rod, don't try to feed the leader through the guides. Double the fly line over and feed it through the guides. This will almost ensure that you won't miss any guides because it's much easier to see and handle. Also, if you drop the line, it will not fall through all the guides, requiring that you start over. I know you're thinking, "What does this have to do with line control?" Line control begins at the truck! The fly line is a tool that we use. It should be used to our advantage not our detriment. Experienced anglers and good

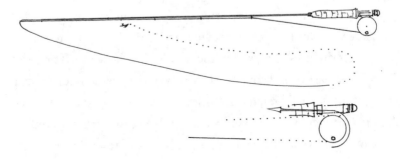

When moving on, keep the fly line out of the end of the rod, place the fly on one of the guides, and wrap the leader around the reel. This ensures you have enough line out of the rod tip to start fishing more quickly. When you're ready to fish, simply take the leader off of the reel and tap the top of your rod. The fly will fall off the guide and you're ready to cast.

fishermen do not spend their time fighting fly line, whether it's at the vehicle or in the water.

GET THE LINE OUT

Once on the stream, get the line out and make a cast. This is a time when I see a lot of anglers struggle. They dip their fly in the water and strip off 6-inch increments of line and hope that the current pulls the line out of their rod tip. As the process drags on, they shake the rod tip and the leader wraps around the tip. This is when they point the tip to me, and I strip off about 6 feet of fly line and drop the fly into the water. The next step is to pull some additional line off the reel for the first cast. They point the rod tip to the sky while they strip the line off their reel, and all of the fly line slides right back down through the guides and lands in a pile at their feet. This doesn't have to happen.

First, when you take the fly off the hook keeper on the rod, hold the fly and pull as much line off the reel as you can reach. When you've reached as far as you can, and the leader is still inside the guides, drop the fly and grab the leader farther up into the butt section and pull again until you have at least a few feet of fly line out of the guides. At this point, drop everything onto the water and strip 8 to 10 feet of line off the reel. At this point, simply take the rod up to the 12 o'clock position and roll cast the line out toward the direction you're going to fish. You can now either begin casting or continue to strip more line off the reel. Either way, the line is out of the rod and you're not going to have any tangles.

MOVING ON

When you're done fishing, point the rod toward the water's surface as you reel in. This will prevent the line from wrapping around the rod tip, as the water surface keeps the line more stable. If you're going to continue to fish, reel in to a point where you still have 3 or 4 feet of line out of the end of your rod tip. Take the fly and place the hook on a guide that is near the end of the rod. Next, take the leader around the reel, and gently reel in the excess line. When you're ready to make your next cast, simply take the line off of the reel and tap the top of your rod. The fly that is hooked on the guide will instantly drop off, and you're ready to fish or strip more line off the reel.

Chapter 6
Lesson Six: Rod Position

If you choose only one common-sense principle from this book to apply to your fishing, I hope it is this one. Good rod position facilitates every technique in this book and its importance cannot be overstated.

Rod position is defined in two ways: The angle at which the rod is held through the drift (which I refer to as pitch) and the relationship that is maintained between the fly and the rod tip throughout the drift. These things together are what allow you to get a drift and be able to set the hook in almost any situation on the trout stream.

If we had 20-foot-long fly rods, we'd always be in the right position. We would never have the issue of fly line laying on the water in multiple currents, pulling our flies all over the place. We would simply be able to place our flies into the water, keep all the line up off the water, and move the rod tip with the current to allow the perfect drift. Unfortunately, this is not reality. So how can we achieve the same result with a 9-foot rod? Well, for starters, we can keep the tip up to keep as much line off the water as possible.

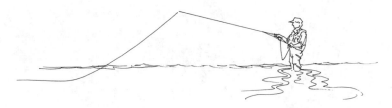

Good rod pitch is paramount to successful fishing. The tip of the rod should never be lower than your shoulders unless you're fishing streamers. A pitch at about the 10 or 10:30 position makes it easier to mend, collect, and pick up line.

Keep the Rod Tip Up

One of the most common problems I see in my guiding is that anglers tend to deliver the cast and then drop the rod tip to the water. The angler at this point has every bit of fly line that is out of the rod in the worst place it can be, the water. There are times and casts where dropping the rod tip is part of a technique, but it is not what I would refer to as a good fishing position. Immediately, the line requires management, and the angler picks the line up and mends it, then drops it right back down into the water, where it will soon need mending again. This is one of the most detrimental habits that I see and one of the hardest to break.

The pitch of the rod is critical to success. Keeping the rod tip up accomplishes several key things. First and most important, an elevated tip keeps less fly line on the water. Fly line on the water will require management. Management requires rod movement, and the less you do of that, the better drift you will get. Second, when a fish takes, you won't have to pick additional line out of the film and do a back flip to set the hook.

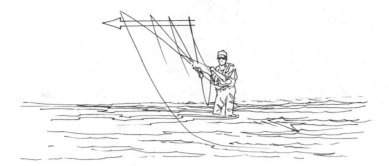

Though the angler is perpendicular to where he's fishing in the stream, the lead and pitch make the corridor between the rod tip to fly parallel to the current. This creates a better drift and a quicker hook-set.

Elevate the rod tip by holding the rod at shoulder height and parallel to the water to keep line off the water. This angle is extremely effective when the rod tip is almost directly above the fly. You can also use the same tip height with the reel slightly lowered to achieve a drift slightly farther away. This method will allow for more line on the water, due to the distance, but still keeps most of the line off the water and allows you to easily manipulate or mend the line that is on the water because of the rod pitch. Once the pitch is set, you can really begin the work with rod position.

Rod Position

Everyone is taught from the very beginning to move the rod with the fly and the current. Some were taught to point the rod right at the fly as it traveled downstream. While this may be a good way to learn to move with the current, it doesn't accomplish a good drift.

Even at farther distances, good pitch allows you to keep most of the fly line off the water, preventing drag and providing a good hooking angle.

Good rod position deals more with the currents than the fly, and the correct position with the rod will eliminate drag.

Never allow the fly line to get below (downstream of) the rod tip. This seems overly simplistic, but applies in almost all cases. There are exceptions to every rule in the book, and on any given day you may come across a piece of water where this principle would not apply. But, by and large, this rule works.

Imagine a corridor approximately three feet wide that extends from the rod tip to the fly. If the fly line is outside of this corridor, you have either mended the line there or the current has pushed the line there. When the current pushes a belly in the line, you must mend the belly to get a drift. This belly spells trouble. You must pick the line up and mend it back upstream, pulling the fly and straightening the leader and put the rod right back in the same position it was in, only to have to do it again. Once this process begins, the drift is essentially over. What ends up happening

Don't allow the fly line to drift below your rod tip (top). Once this occurs, it is nearly impossible to achieve a drag-free drift or set the hook efficiently. As the line drifts back toward you, slowly lift the rod tip to pick up the slack. You can then roll cast the slack back toward the fly.

is your flies are only fishable a small percentage of the time they are in the water and catch rates drop substantially.

What can be done to improve this? Change the rod position. Unless you are fishing directly upstream, the rod should be moving with the current. The pitch should stay as fixed as possible, but the direction of the rod should move with the speed of the water. I see anglers struggle constantly with their mends as they keep the rod in the same position and try to mend the line by pulling and yanking it into a different place. In many cases, they are not even mending the problem area; they are simply moving the line directly in front of the rod. If the problem area (the belly) is not in between the rod tip and the fly, the attempted mend will do nothing more than straighten the leader and ruin the drift.

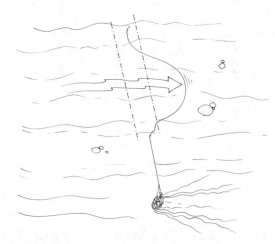

When a downstream belly forms in your line, the line is out of the corridor (represented by the dotted lines). When this occurs, mending the line without straightening the leader is nearly impossible. In this illustration, the rod is in the wrong position to correct the problem.

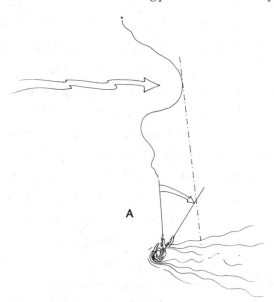

To mend effectively in this situation, the rod tip must be moved downstream of the problem area (A). This creates a new corridor from which you can make a good mend and continue the drag-free drift.

Have you ever noticed that the first mend you make immediately after the cast is always your best? That's because the rod is naturally in the right position to execute the mend properly. Keep the fly line in the corridor. Move the rod tip so that the fly line stays between the tip and the fly. This will not only improve the drift, but it will enable a better mend. If the fly line is 5 or 6 feet downstream, outside of the corridor, you can't mend the line from the corridor. You have to move the rod tip to a position downstream of the problem area (the belly), thus creating a new corridor in order to effectively mend the line. You can easily mend from the correct position with the correct pitch, rod tip, and wrist. Trying to mend line that is outside of the corridor is fruitless.

The Corridor

The corridor is defined by the fly on one end and the rod tip on the other. If there were a flood light placed on the rod tip and it pointed toward the fly, the beam of light would be a good representation of the corridor. The corridor serves two distinctly different purposes. First, it defines the limits by which an effective mend can be made. If the current is allowed to push the fly line too far outside of the boundaries of this corridor, a mend cannot be applied to the drift. You define the corridor with the position of the rod tip. You have control to the point of how far you can reach with the tip, and you should get into position in the stream where you can maximize your drifts.

The second and primary purpose of the corridor is that it is the area where you should keep your slack. The objective is to create the proper amount of slack and control it in a specified area (the corridor). In order to get the proper drift, there has to be a certain amount of slack, but great anglers are able to use the least amount of slack possible that still allows for a good drift. Vince Marinaro once said, "If it's small, black, and unattached, they'll eat it." I often repeat this quote to my clients. The rod tip moves with the fastest moving part of the fly line, and you continually throw mends, in the form of a mini-roll cast, right at the end of the fly line. In some instances, there may be a flip of the line in one direction or another, but the mends are small and continuous throughout the drift. The important advantage here is that all of the slack is in one plane in between the tip and the fly, which allows you to quickly pick up line and come tight to a fish. Additionally, this keeps the slack to a minimum. If you place the slack in the corridor, there is not a need for a lot of extra line and it is much easier to manage.

Good rod position will eliminate nearly all issues when fishing close. If you are fishing less than 20 feet of line, you should seldom have to make a mend. When fishing a line of current with a dry fly

You can fish effectively even if you are perpendicular to the current by minimizing the amount of line on the water and moving the rod tip at the same speed as the current.

or nymph, try to fish so that the tip of the rod to the fly is parallel to the current line. Perpendicular is okay, as long as the line is off of the water and the rod tip is moving at the exact speed of the current. If the line is in the water, a drift will only be achieved if all of the current is one speed. Otherwise, you must mend to achieve the drift.

Although the angler and the fly rod may be perpendicular to the run, the line between the rod tip and the fly is what needs to be parallel. Use the length of the fly rod and either position the rod tip completely vertical to the run, or downstream of the run. In any case, make the corridor parallel to the current. I tell my clients to lead the flies through the run with the rod tip. This doesn't mean to pull the flies, but it's very close.

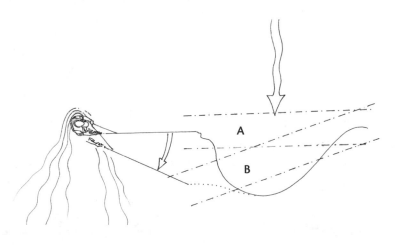

Mending this belly with the rod in the original position **(A)** *will do nothing but straighten the leader and ruin the drift. By simply moving the rod into a better position to make this mend and changing the corridor* **(B),** *the mend becomes effortless.*

Chapter 7
Lesson Seven: Mending

Controlled slack may have been a better title to this chapter, but most anglers identify with the term mending, so that is what we're going to use. Mending line is a necessary evil on most of the water we fish. If you're like me and you have a tendency to fish close, rod position alone can eliminate mending a lot of the time. However, most fishing situations require us, at least part of the time, to fish at distances that aren't so close. To be able to accomplish this successfully, we need to be able to manipulate the line and create drifts at distances beyond the rod tip.

Mending is the act of manipulating the fly line into a position on the stream's surface so that it will not influence the speed of the fly or indicator. This is usually accomplished by flipping the fly line upstream of the fly or indicator once you cast. In a perfect world, all of the current is one speed and everything flows at the exact speed of the current, achieving a perfect drift. In the real world, there are multiple current speeds, and the fly line is swept away and is moving downstream almost immediately. If this line is not moved to a position upstream of the fly, the tension on the line from the current will immediately drag the fly.

When executed properly, a roll cast mend uses minimal slack, doesn't move the fly, and helps achieve a good drag-free drift by throwing slack up toward the fly.

Anglers will typically pick the rod tip up, and with one big sweeping motion, pull the fly line upstream to try and negate the effect of the current. This technique produces a good drift for a limited distance, and if there happens to be a trout there looking to eat, you may catch it. But this method often takes all of the slack out of the line and leader. Once that happens, your chances of catching a trout become slim.

With correct rod position, mending is not difficult. It is important to strip line in when necessary, and never have too much line out of the rod. Most important, it should not be a process that takes a bunch of line from one bad place and puts it in another. It should be an act of relocating line and eliminating it from the drift.

Controlling the slack that you do not need for a good drift is paramount. Too much slack leads to less control on the hook-set, possible drag, and too much line to pick up and re-cast. In many instances, the fly will be drifting closer, and after your initial mend, you will almost always need to gather some slack line before you mend again. I see lots of one-handed fishermen throughout the year. They're usually the guys that have a fat cigar in one hand while they fish. They make their cast and try to manage all the line with a series of mends without ever stripping any line through the drift. This is not an effective way to fish, and I always tell those guys that fly fishing is a two-handed sport.

Casting

The fly line has a huge surface area and is responsible for 90 percent of our drift problems. To fish effectively, you must be able to control where the fly line is at all times during the drift, and this control begins with the cast. Begin by assessing the drift before you make the cast and determine where the fly line needs to land in addition to where the fly needs to be. Keep the fly line in a manageable location. So often, by the time you realize that you need to mend it is too late and when you do mend, you end up ruining the drift. Be prepared to deal with tricky currents and be proactive by using a cast that places the fly line at or above the fly in the current.

REACH CAST

The reach cast is commonly used when casting to a target across a strong current. If you cast straight across stream, your fly line would drag immediately. To combat this, stop the forward stroke aimed at the target as you would normally, but then move the rod horizontally, left or right (without changing the pitch), so that the fly line lands upstream of the fly, which buys you time for any necessary mends. Often, the reach cast alone is enough for a good drift.

Although you are still casting directly at the target, you must cast more line than you would usually use for a cast straight across stream because you need the extra line as you reach upstream. A reach cast with the same amount of line that you would use to make a straight, across-stream cast is ineffective and often short of the target. Whenever you introduce slack into your presentation,

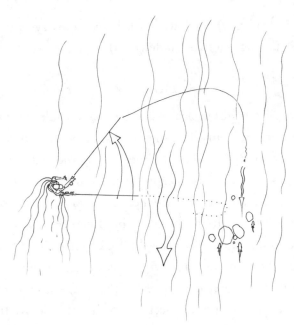

The reach cast is a proactive approach to combating drag. As the fly reaches the target, the slack is perfectly aligned in the corridor where you can make another mend to extend the drift.

whether during the cast in the case of the reach or after the cast in the case of a mend, you need to use more line.

After the reach cast, the corridor has been established and the line should be in perfect position. To keep the rod tip at the end of the corridor, move it downstream so the line does not belly outside of the corridor. When you can no longer reach with the rod, mend the line upstream with the rod tip by using a sharp snap of the wrist to buy more time. This should not move the fly, but if it does it will be slight, and your good drift will continue. Repeat this when necessary. Be careful not to over mend. You should never have more line out of the end of your rod than is absolutely necessary to get a good drift. Remember, if the fly line is on the water, it can only cause problems, so only use as much as is absolutely necessary to get the drift.

SLACK-LEADER CAST

Another example of controlled slack is the slack-leader cast. This one also requires more line than the typical cast. As outlined earlier, this cast is thrown high and shocked, so that slack is built into the leader and fly line. When this cast lands, you can immediately begin collecting and mending line without moving the fly.

Once you mend, collect the additional slack underneath your index finger and let it hang right there. I always have a few feet, sometimes more, hanging off my reel so that I can introduce slack into the drift or extend a cast. Either way, it won't hurt you as long as it's behind the trigger finger.

Rod Position

When fishing straight upstream, or nearly straight upstream, you must still consider the corridor. While it is much easier to keep the fly line within the side boundaries of the corridor, you must make sure that the line does not travel downstream of the end of the corridor marked by the rod tip. A huge loop of line downstream of the rod tip prevents you from efficiently setting the hook on a trout because most, if not all, of your energy is used to pick up all the excess line downstream of you.

To prevent this, it is critical that you maintain proper rod pitch. Upon delivering the cast, keep the pitch between 10:30 and 11 o'clock. As the fly and line drift toward you, raise the rod tip to pick up the line collecting at your feet. In slower currents, you would normally strip this line under the index finger, but in faster

Once a belly forms below the rod tip, the drift is essentially over. As you collect or move line, you will undoubtedly pull the fly and create drag. Fortunately, this is easily correctable through better rod position (below).

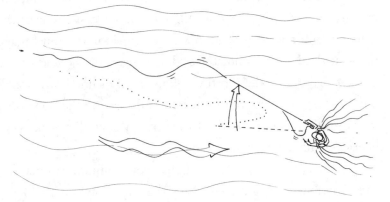

To prevent this detrimental belly in the line, move the rod tip downstream of the problem, where you can throw a roll-cast mend toward the fly, or simply collect the line as it drifts toward you.

currents, this is not possible. In both cases, simply stripping and collecting the line once a loop of line collects below the rod tip will pull the fly.

You can overcome this problem by using some of the slack that is drifting toward you to make a miniature roll cast that throws all of the slack back toward the fly, between the fly and the rod tip. As the fly and the slack are drifting toward you, simply raise the rod tip and sharply execute the miniature roll between the 10:30 and 9 o'clock position straight ahead so that the slack never has a chance to get downstream of the rod tip. After each roll cast, quickly strip out the slack without moving the fly. As this is occurring, the fly is still drifting toward you, creating more slack. Repeat this process until you are ready to make another cast, but do not overdo it.

Downstream Mends

Sometimes you must mend line into the current to get a drift, such as when you cast into currents that are faster than those you are standing in. Often, to achieve a good drift, you must mend

A roll-cast mend relocates the slack in the drift closer to the fly. Pick up the rod tip slightly as the fly drifts back to you, and instead of stripping in that slack, throw it toward the end of the fly line.

the line into the faster current, or downstream. Once again, rod position is important. Don't try to mend outside of the corridor. Point the rod at the problem area and move the line. Once the line has been moved, a new corridor has been created because the rod position has changed. Whenever possible, keep the corridor between the rod tip and the fly parallel to the current. A mend of this type often requires a second upstream mend. Mend as often as necessary to achieve the drift.

Long-Line Mends

Without a 20-foot rod, it is not always possible to keep the corridor parallel to the current. At times, you have to fish straight across stream, and across several currents. To get a good drift, you have to pick the line up and mend it. Most anglers can mend 15 or 20 feet of line without a problem but have considerably more difficulty when working with 30 or 40 feet. At these distances, rod position and technique really come into play.

In order to mend 30 feet or more of fly line, the rod tip must first be at or below the problem area. In other words, if there is a belly in the line, the rod must be ahead of the problem area in order to pick it up. If the stream is flowing left to right and the cast is delivered across stream, a belly will occur in the fly line from the rod to the fly. Typically, the angler will pick the line up slowly and in a sweeping motion to the left attempt to relocate the line into an upstream belly to allow time for the drift to occur.

In my guiding I see this often and what generally happens is that the angler only mends half the line, creating a large S in the water, and the problem is never really fixed. The belly that was not mended still pulls on the fly, but the angler feels as though he did

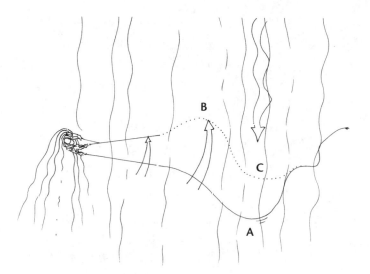

Once a belly forms in the line **(A),** *a mend made with poor rod position only affects the line that is right in front of the angler* **(B)** *and doesn't remove the belly below the fly* **(C).** *It is common for anglers to continue to mend this way without ever solving the problem.*

the right thing in making the mend. Additionally, the slow motion and pull on the line to make the mend has completely straightened out the leader. This is a bad recipe for a good drift.

If your mend takes all the slack out of the leader and line, it didn't do what it was supposed to do. In this situation, you must mend all the line. The pitch should be at the 10:30 position, and the correct rod position can be located by placing the rod tip at the end of an imaginary line that begins at the fly and extends through the lowest point downstream of the fly line (which is the belly, and the problem area). Once you move your rod tip to this point, execute a sharp roll cast right toward, and slightly upstream of, the fly. This is done using only the rod tip with a motion between 12 and 10:30

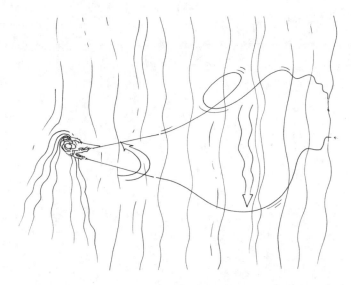

When you mend, make sure you move all of the line. Move the rod downstream of the problem area and keep the tip up. With minimal rod movement, not a big sweeping motion, snap your wrist sharply and throw slack toward the end of the fly line with the tip of the rod, without straightening the leader.

that throws the excess line upstream of the fly. Executed properly, this mend will not move the indicator or fly and will maintain the slack that is already in the leader. Sometimes in order to make this cast effectively, a little extra slack is required, and I will often shake a little extra line out of the end of the rod.

Proactive Mending

The final key to mending is simply knowing when to do it. Your ability to anticipate the need for a mend before a problem arises can be the key to success. Manipulating the line is easiest when there is little or no pressure on it from the current. You will eventually learn the appropriate measures that you need to take after one or two drifts through an area. This ability to anticipate will come with experience, but practice and knowledge will take years off the learning curve.

After you thoroughly fish a stretch of water, take a few minutes and practice getting a good drift in all the areas you're able to reach. Any stretch of water will present enough challenges to be worth the time. Practice will speed up your learning time, and who knows, you may even catch one.

Part Two
Putting the
Lessons Together

Chapter 8
Nymphing

Nymphing is where the rubber meets the road. Trout do the vast majority of their feeding under the surface, so to catch them consistently throughout the year, you have to fish subsurface. Because of this simple fact, nymphing accounts for the majority of fish caught in any given year, and to be a good fly fisherman, you have to be a good nymph fisherman.

I rarely fish a dry fly without seeing convincing evidence that I should be fishing on top. I throw nymphs at fish that are not feeding consistently. An occasional rise won't do it for me. An occasional rise only means that a fish is looking to eat, not necessarily that he wants to eat on the surface. Except for rare cases, the best fish are almost always caught under the surface. Rising puts the trout at risk from predators and takes energy; a meal delivered under the surface to a fish that wants to eat will almost always produce if presented properly.

Fishing under the surface has other advantages as well. I have found that trout tend to be less discriminating about their choice of food when little or no risk is involved in eating. At any given time in a trout stream, there are hundreds of options for the trout and if the right depth and drift are achieved, they will often eat whatever is presented. That being said, there are certainly times when the menu is full of a particular insect, such as Sulphurs, and it makes perfect sense to throw what is most prevalent. In my experience, a good selection of generic nymphs in different sizes and colors will do the trick in any trout stream from Pennsylvania to Montana.

High-Stick Nymphing

Trout are opportunistic feeders. Unlike bass, they don't spend their time on the prowl looking for food, and they don't spend the majority of their time feeding. They sit on the bottom conserving energy, staying safe, and taking what food is made available to them through the current. They are good at hiding, and so anglers have to learn what type of water they like and what type of conditions will produce good holding areas. Often, the areas that look best are tough to reach and seem to be in places that would be impossible to get a fly deep enough to reach the fish. High-stick nymphing, or deep nymphing, is the one method I choose for just this scenario.

High-sticking is a form of nymphing where the corridor between the fly and the rod tip is at a near 90-degree angle to the bottom of the stream. Because the rod tip is almost directly above the fly, and the rod tip, line, and fly all move at the same speed as the current, the nymphs get deep quickly.

To high-stick effectively, you need to be able to reach over the top of the fly, or at least be able to keep all of the fly line off of the water, which limits its effectiveness to within 15 or 20 feet of the targeted area. I prefer to be directly across from, or slightly below (downstream) the target. The corridor now has two dimensions:

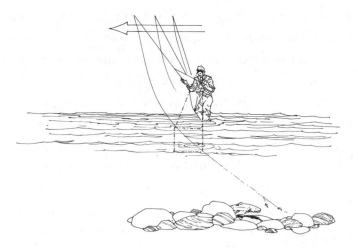

A slight lead creates an angle, which in turn provides an accurate way to detect any movement in the rig. The key to success is to create a consistent angle throughout the drift, so that even the slightest change in speed will be discernible.

The vertical dimension, which is defined by the distance between the fly and the rod tip, and the horizontal dimension, which is defined by the lead, or how far downstream the rod tip is from the fly.

When the rod tip is slightly ahead of the fly on the bottom, a slight amount of slack is created in the leader that is out of the water that you can use as an indicator. The key to success with this system is to create a consistent angle and view of the leader (what I call a sight picture) throughout the entire drift, so that even the slightest change in speed will be discernible.

WEIGHT

High-stick nymphing works because it eliminates excess line and gets the fly on the bottom. If you don't feel the bottom, add more weight. If there's one thing I've learned over the years, it's that if you're not catching fish when nymphing, it's usually not the choice of nymphs you're fishing, it is more likely that you're not deep enough. Never be afraid to add more weight.

Just this past season, my client Steve and I were high-sticking a run that I knew held a lot of trout. It was at the head of a fairly strong riffle and the depth was only about two feet. This particular run is very predictable. If the fish are not in the lower section of it, you can always find them in the head until later in the season when they completely disappear from the stretch. This is like clockwork, and it never lets me down. Except today. I couldn't explain it. We were right where they were supposed to be, and not a single take. I had three #4 split-shot on, and Steve was doing everything right.

As I was exploring options and buying time to figure out where I was going to go next, the thought occurred to me that Steve hadn't hung up a single time. Now this is a situation where the dropping water level actually made getting to the bottom more difficult because of the speed of the current rushing over the rocks. There were fewer pockets to suck the fly into, and the right amount of weight last week was not the right amount today. I'd love to tell you that I recognized that fact as I was standing there, but I can't. I put another shot on and after several drifts, still did not reach the bottom. I told Steve to say goodbye to the flies as I placed yet another #4 shot onto the leader, and after several more good drifts, he was finally picking up moss on the flies at the end of the drift. I eventually put one more shot on after the drifts produced nothing and that was the ticket. With seven #4 shot on the leader, we eventually pulled four fish out of the two-foot-deep run.

So, how do you know how much shot to start out with? That depends on current and depth. I always recommend starting light and increasing the weight as you go. I prefer a lot of small shot to a couple of larger shot, but I have no scientific reason for that other than you can add and take off smaller increments of weight to get the exact amount that you need. I prefer shot to lead putty because the weight of shot is consistent, and I can usually look at a piece of water and have a good idea of how much weight I'll need. Where legal, I prefer to fish lead shot over tin. Tin shot is not as heavy as lead and it tends to fall off the leader more easily than lead.

Because bottom currents are often slower than surface currents (sometimes significantly slower), if you do not have enough weight, the flies not only don't get down, they move through the run too quickly. I'm always amazed when I finally get enough shot on the line and the drift slows down. This is when you start to catch fish.

TUCK CAST

I have taught hundreds of anglers to high-stick. You don't have to be a world-class caster, and you don't have to be able to mend 40 feet of line. It begins with a cast that gets the fly deep fast. I use the tuck cast, developed by the late George Harvey and made famous by his protégé Joe Humphreys. This cast uses a lot of power through the forward stroke and has an abrupt stop that shocks the leader and bounces the fly and weight straight down into the water. This breaks through the surface film quickly and the fly immediately sinks to the bottom.

After the cast, hold the rod tip up, keeping all of the line off the water. At close range, the rod tip is almost directly over the flies; at longer range, all the line is still held off of the surface with a slight arc in the fly line that can be used as a strike indicator. Then, strip the excess line through your finger on the rod hand, so no fly line touches the surface of the water, and keep the rod tip slightly ahead of the flies, leading them through the water you are fishing. The absence of fly line or leader on the surface facilitates the sinking process immensely.

As soon as you strip in the excess line within the first two to three seconds of the delivery, the rod pitch is set, and the relationship between the rod tip and the point of entry at the water is now locked. This should not change through the drift, and the sooner this is established, the better.

LEADING THE DRIFT

Now, at this point, everything moves together with the current. The rod tip should be slightly ahead of the fly, in the same line of current. It should be leading the fly, but not pulling it. This is very important. If the rod tip does not have the correct positioning, two detrimental factors occur. The first is that an accurate sight picture is never established. If the rod tip is behind the point of entry, there is nothing to gauge the drift by. In other words, if the drift is completely vertical, in order for you to see anything happening to the leader, the rod would have to continue to move forward before it would be discernible. The trout is doing nothing more than opening its mouth and accepting the fly. You have to be able to see everything and anything. Often, this is too late and the fish will spit the fly. If the rod is positioned slightly forward, everything that the fly touches will be visible.

The second detrimental effect that is caused by poor positioning is that the fly never reaches its maximum depth. If the rod tip trails the fly, or is directly above the fly, a bow forms in the leader between the fly and where the leader enters the water. This seems very slight, but it makes a tremendous difference. I have often

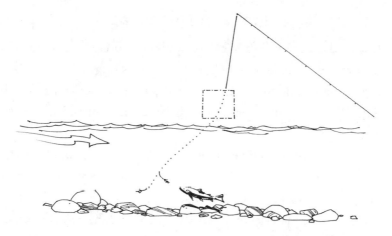

This sight box is critical to your nymphing success. You must be able to discern a strike in this area, so pay particular attention to the lead. A slight lead with the rod tip will detect a strike much better than a vertical position.

worked with clients trying to get the right lead in a run where I knew there were fish that we just were not able to reach. Drift after drift would prove fruitless until the first time they got the lead right. As soon as that happened, we'd snag bottom. I was compensating for the poor lead with weight. As soon as they got the lead, we'd go straight to the bottom and lose the flies. It makes a big difference.

Hook set is the third reason why this lead is important. The lead, when executed properly, requires little more than a slight lift to connect with the trout. The set downstream comes more naturally because of the lead. Trout face upstream, yet many anglers instinctively set upstream, pulling the hook away from the fish. The proper lead in high-stick nymphing makes a set downstream, into the trout's mouth, almost automatic.

Indicator Nymphing

Just as the key to high-stick nymphing is to create a good sight picture, the same holds true for indicator fishing. The key to success is being able to set the rig up so that the take is discernible. After that, you must get a good drift in the right places, at the right depth.

Fishing with an indicator is probably the most popular method of nymph fishing. Walk into any fly shop and you'll see many different indicators that all work. What distinguishes one from another is the material they're made out of and the way they attach to your line. For the most part, they all float pretty well. What I look for in an indicator is ease of movement. I see many anglers that set their rig up to begin fishing and never change the location of the indicator. This is not using the rig effectively. As a general rule, the indicator should be set at 1 ½ times the depth of the

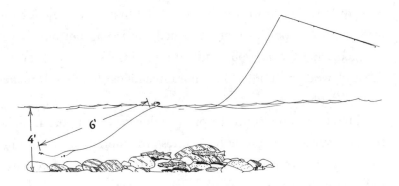

A general rule of thumb is to set the indicator up the leader 1 ½ times the depth of the water. This allows the flies to drift freely without being influenced by the indicator and provides a proper lead that allows you to detect the take.

water you are fishing. If you're fishing 4 feet of water, the indicator should be placed 6 feet up the leader from the fly. This is to allow the fly to sink, and not impede the drift. This also forms the proper lead that will allow you to detect a take quicker.

My favorite type of indicator is putty. It's easy to move or take off and it's biodegradable if you lose it while casting. I tie my own leaders and it works well to attach the putty to a knot, but it does not stick that well to prefabricated leaders. Other types of indicators work well with all kinds of leaders, but they put a set in the leader that never comes out. If you don't mind this liability, pick one that you can move and see, and you'll be fine.

When fishing an indicator rig, keep your loops open. You don't want to try to throw a tight loop, especially with some of the bigger indicators. They are highly wind-resistant and will create nothing but trouble. Also, minimize the number of false casts. There is no reason to ever false-cast a nymph rig more than twice. I have had clients over the years that spent more time false-casting than fishing, and any guide will tell you that is one of the most frustrating things on the planet. False casts are used in nymphing for two reasons—changing direction and increasing distance. Other than that, they are unnecessary and will cause more problems than they're worth.

Nymphing with an indicator uses a lot of the same practices as high-sticking. The major difference between the two is that an indicator rig can cover a lot more water from a distance. Close in, you should use the same method as high-sticking. Attempt to keep all the line to the indicator off the water, when possible, and maintain the same lead and pitch with the rod tip. As the fishing extends farther away from you, the rules of the corridor begin to play a major role. It is here that rod position and pitch are even more valuable, as the need for mending begins to play an important part in the drift. Line management skills come into play as well with collecting and creating slack.

CONTROLLED SLACK

All too often, I watch anglers mend immediately following the cast and consequently they never have any slack built into the drift. The line is tight from the cast, and their first mend pulls out any slack that was naturally built into the leader. To create a controlled amount of slack in the presentation to make mends and adjustments without moving the indicator, once the indicator settles onto the water allow it to drift momentarily to create some slack. Keep a 10:30 pitch on the rod and maintain the corridor, keeping the line in between the rod tip and the indicator.

As the indicator drifts downstream, you can lift the rod tip to 12 o'clock without moving the indicator by using the slack that is

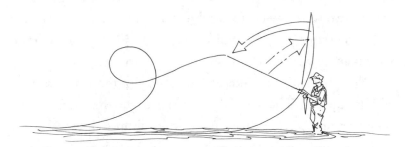

When working with a longer line, bring the rod tip back to the 12 o'clock position in order to facilitate the roll-cast mend. If you need extra slack to throw into the mend, it sometimes helps to take it from the reel.

being produced as the indicator drifts downstream. Make a sharp roll cast directed right at the indicator or slightly upstream of it between 12 o'clock and 10:30 to throw slack to the end of the fly line slightly above, or right at, the indicator. A second mend may be necessary to the middle of the fly line, but is easily accomplished with the right pitch on the rod. Strip in the excess line and continue the process as the indicator and flies drift downstream. This exercise makes the fly fishable through the entire drift and will double your fishing time.

The corridor between the rod tip and the indicator is your area of operation. You can control everything that happens in that defined area with the correct rod pitch and position. Don't allow the stream to dictate how you fish, create the drift. Once you master this method, you can achieve a drift in almost any situation and keep the flies fishable throughout the entire process.

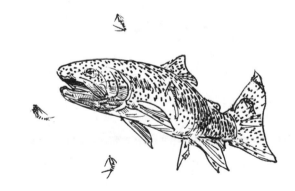

Chapter 9
Dry-Fly Fishing

Evening is beginning to settle in as the last bit of warmth from the sun disappears over the ridge. The entire river is now shaded, and a cool breeze makes me wish I had packed a fleece in my vest. The flat I am wading is below a long riffle, and it's been like a sheet of glass for the past hour. If I didn't know better, I would swear it was void of life. I have fished the entire day and landed a total of three fish, jagged a few others, and lost one good one early this morning before the sun got up. It had to have reached 90 degrees without a cloud in the sky.

The water is low and clear, about the way it should be toward the end of May, and if it weren't for the limestone water, it would surely be too warm. As it is, this is quite normal for this time of year, and the tough fishing today is nothing more than a reflection of how good the fishing is throughout the evenings. The trout don't need to feed during the day; they get their food delivered in the evenings, right about dusk.

As time passes on, I notice the birds starting to stage up in the trees that line the banks of the river. I begin to see a few Sulphurs here and there, an occasional Cahill, a March Brown, several caddis, and lots of crane flies. The first rises appear on the far side of the river, right on the bank. These fish are often not catchable. They are sporadic, and not on any one particular insect. They're excited.

I've learned over the years to not start casting to the first rises I see. This only froths the water and prevents the fish from staging where they want to for the event. Instead, I pick my position, set up, and wait. I've chosen my location after years of fishing this hatch in this river, and I know there will be some large trout rising straight across stream from me. I will wait until they are comfortable enough to start rising consistently.

The bugs begin to get heavy, and almost instantaneously the trout get on them. I haven't moved a muscle in almost 20 minutes, and I have a 9-inch trout feeding five feet in front of me. I watch him as I keep an eye on the bank for the big boys. A stoic-looking March Brown drifts right into the small trout's lane. To my surprise, the little fish surfaces slowly and drifts with the insect for nearly two feet before deciding not to eat it, and descends back to his holding area. I watch the bug continue drifting downstream, thinking to myself this was his lucky day, when a 4-inch trout comes completely out of the water and devours the insect. I continue to watch the little 9-inch fish as he is now staged just under the surface.

A struggling Sulphur approaches on its side, trying to free its wings. The little trout takes it with vengeance, throwing water as though there were a struggle. Out of the corner of my eye, I see a heavy boil on the bank. I've yet to tie a fly on my leader because, as things go, you never really know what they're going to be eating. My first instinct would have been to fish a Sulphur dun, but I am now seeing spinners and I'm sure that the big trout on the bank that I'm targeting is eating exactly that. The spinners are dancing above the riffles, a hundred yards upstream of me, and are falling to the surface and being washed to the edge of the stream. The big boys like to sit right on the edge where there is no current, because they can lazily sip spinners from now until the sun comes up.

I tie a Sulphur spinner onto 6X tippet and wait for the next rise. As I'm waiting for a target, I notice spinners all over the water, and hundreds of fish are rising. I back out of my position so that I can catch a few trout before I go for the trophies. This is clearly a rookie move, but I can't help myself. I really want to see if the pattern I'm using for the spinner is going to work.

The first fish I cast to takes the spinner with no hesitation, and I quickly land a beautiful 13-inch wild brownie. I have easily 20 fish that I can cast to from my position, and I decide on one that has risen three times in the past ten seconds. I land the spinner pattern six inches upstream of his last rise, and I'm immediately connected to the second fish. I keep watching the bank after I release the fish, and there are two really good fish pac-manning spinners in water so shallow their backs nearly breach the water.

I cast to the first trout that was the farthest upstream, so that hopefully I could pull him out into the current and not disturb the other feeders. The first drift was dead on, and though I couldn't see my fly by this time, I knew it was in the general vicinity. When the giant mouth displaced water in the twilight up underneath the hemlocks, I set the hook. The fight was on! Water splashed all over the bank, and I could not pull him anywhere. He was going to stay wherever he wanted, and after he thrashed around there and destroyed any chance of fishing there later, he shot off upstream. After an epic ten-minute battle on light tippet, I landed the 19-inch wild brown and was done for the evening.

Fooling a trout on a dry fly may be the ultimate victory in the game of fly fishing. Perhaps it is because you see the take, or because of the challenge inherent in making the fly float properly and appear like a real insect. I have caught many fish in my lifetime, and have been a part of the process with hundreds and hundreds of clients over the years, and the most memorable fish are always caught on dry flies.

The Searching Drift

Searching drifts are longer than drifts targeted for specific risers. When I use a dry fly to search for trout, it is often during low, clear water. This is rare for me. As I mentioned earlier, I prefer to fish nymphs most often, but there are times when I believe the trout will be looking up and may even move a good distance to eat something off the surface. Later in the season, when these conditions usually occur, I will typically fish a caddis or terrestrial such as a beetle or ant. At these times, you have a much better chance of fooling the fish if they do not know you are there, which means long, upstream casts. I will often stand in the center of the stream, if possible, and work upstream, paying particular attention to the edges.

When covering the water and searching with dry flies, begin by fishing the water you're about to step into, and then get in. Distance between you and the fish is often more important than fly pattern or drift, but start by casting close. You may find that you don't need to fish far away to catch them. If you're not hooking up, extend the distance you cast upstream, covering every inch of likely looking water. I like to be able to fish 20 to 30 feet upstream, and that is the area that I focus on. When my fly finishes drifting through that target area, I pick up and recast. One of the advantages of fly fishing is that we don't have to reel all of the line in to begin the next cast. So don't waste time letting your flies drift all the way back to you when your target is 30 feet upstream. Stay targeted and focused.

Casting to Risers

Few things in fly fishing are more fun than casting to rising trout. For one thing, half the battle is over because you've found a fish and you know it is eating. All you have to do is select the right pattern and drift it to the fish. Piece of cake, right?

The beauty of targeted surface action is that you really only need three feet of drift. This is by far the best practice you'll ever have for casting and drifting. There's an instant reward if you do it right. However, I have often said that this is like golf. Sometimes you make a great shot to get to the green, and then you four putt. It's the great shot that brings you back.

Casting to risers requires tight loops. Why? So that everything lands on the water at the same time. Fly, line, and leader must be able to be placed properly in the current to allow for the short drift. Wide loops tend to drop the fly line first, and the line

When choosing which rising fish to cast to, look for one that is rising consistently. Sporadic risers frustrate even expert anglers because they are not feeding on the surface heavily and may be moving too much.

is swept away by the current as the fly slowly descends, straightening the leader and ruining your drift before you even begin. Tight loops also allow you to shock the leader if necessary to create additional slack by abruptly stopping the forward cast so that the leader actually bounces back on itself slightly into a series of coils, thus allowing a longer drift.

When choosing a fish to cast to, look for one that is rising consistently. Sporadic risers will frustrate even the best fishermen, so stay away from them. Don't waste your valuable fishing time. Find a fish that is feeding steadily, and staying still. If you put him down, pick another fish. If you get several good drifts over a fish and he hasn't eaten, consider changing your pattern. My instinct is usually to go smaller, and most often I hang an emerger off the dry.

The drift to a rising fish is created in the cast and the rod position. The slack, mend (if necessary), and the drift is completely set up by the time the cast lands. The drift should begin one to two feet upstream of the fish and extend just beyond the fish. After that, you should softly pick up the line and cast again to the same location. Trout feed in a rhythm. Sometimes our drift doesn't fit into it. The more times a trout sees the fly, the better shot you have of catching it.

Leader Design

Aside from accuracy and the ability to make slack line and reach casts, leaders are one of the most important aspects of dry-fly fishing, because it is the delivery mechanism that controls the amount of slack, aside from the fly line. Especially important with small flies, a poorly designed leader will make a good drift nearly impossible. In dry-fly fishing, drag that is imperceptible to the eye, or micro drag, is a major consideration.

I have often watched anglers change pattern after pattern in the last light of day, thinking they had the wrong imitation on the end of their line, when the fact was they weren't getting a drift. Their last-ditch effort is a larger pattern that they can see in the fading light, and because the larger bug doesn't get twisted, pulled, and turned by the faulty leader, they catch a trout.

I have always used a Harvey leader formula for my fishing and specifications and tips for proper leader construction are in the next chapter on page 100. Not only does the Harvey-style leader introduce the amount of slack necessary for a drag-free drift, but by using the same formula and length, I can be consistent in my casting, which is extremely hard to do with prefabricated leaders, especially as you add tippets to them. I build my dry-fly leaders from monofilament. Not only is fluorocarbon extremely expensive, but it sinks and it is stiffer than mono, two properties that are not conducive to good drifts with a surface-floating fly.

I'll discuss leader to fly line connections in the next chapter in more detail, but the connection is an important consideration for delicate dry-fly presentations. I like to use a nail knot because I feel that it transfers energy of the fly line to the leader better than any other connection plus it has the slimmest profile, which reduces the chances of it disturbing the water, both on the pick-up and the presentation casts. Many anglers will nail-knot a piece of heavy mono to their fly line and place a loop on it, which they then attach their leader to with a loop-to-loop connection. I still prefer a direct knotted connection to the fly line, and a simple blood knot between the heavy mono and the leader will perform more consistently. Monofilament that is too heavy, like .024-inch diameter, on a 4- or 5-weight line creates a hinge point right at the connection that will stress and weaken the fly line over time.

Chapter 10
Rigs for Success

F ly rigs are as individual as the people who put them together. Every angler has his own way of doing things, and though I would never suggest that there is a right or wrong way to rig, I do believe that some methods are better than others. While riggings starts where you attach the backing on the reel spool, I am going to talk about the business end in this chapter—everything after the point where the leader is attached to the fly line.

Leaders

I would be willing to bet that fewer than 10 percent of all fly fishermen tie their own leaders. This is too bad because the leader, as the late George Harvey once said, is the most important part of your tackle. Once, while teaching a clinic with Joe Humphreys, I mentioned to him that the leaders I was seeing were atrocious. I commented, "Is anyone teaching these kids anything about leaders? Does anyone understand what the leader is supposed to do?" I was not happy about what I was seeing, and Joe, not to my surprise, threw his hands up and agreed.

A properly designed leader should turn over and collapse the tippet section into a series of coils on the water that allow a perfect drag-free drift. The leader is not supposed to turn over and straighten out. If this happens, as soon as the current grabs the fly line and begins to take it away, the fly will drag immediately.

If you really want to become an accurate caster, you need to use a consistent leader. The leader, if constructed properly and attached correctly, will deposit the fly in the exact same place every cast, providing the cast is the same. Store-bought extruded leaders are inconsistent at best and once you begin to use them and break them, they are impossible to work on. They will never perform like a tied leader.

The leader to fly line connection also affects accuracy. We have a hundred variables at play every time we make a cast. Why make one more with a faulty connection? Loop-to-loop connections do not provide a smooth transfer of energy from the line to the leader and for light-line trout fishing can be a liability with the extra disturbance they create on the surface, both when picking line up and laying it down. A nail knot takes 20 seconds to tie and it performs better than anything else I have tried.

The Reverse Clinch

I use three knots the most: the nail knot, blood knot, and clinch (or improved clinch). I use the nail knot to attach leader to fly line, and the blood knot for attaching two pieces of tippet or leader that are different diameters. Many anglers find the triple surgeon's knot easier to tie, though I think it is bulkier than the blood knot. You can find illustrations of all of these knots in books or online, so I won't cover them here.

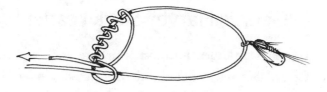

Pass the tippet through the top of the hook eye with your left hand
(directions are for a right-handed person). We'll call the tippet in front
of the hook eye the standing line. With the thumb and forefinger of
your right hand, grasp the working end of the tippet so that three
inches extend beyond your fingers (the tag), allowing the fly to hang
freely. Turn up the palm of your right hand so that the fly is against the
back of your fingers. Pinching both the standing line and the working
line with your left hand, wrap the tag end of the tippet around the
standing line and tie a five-turn clinch knot.

Hold the remaining tag with the left hand and expand the fingers of
the right hand inside the loop, cinching the knot tight.

Clip the tag and then pull the knot down to the fly by pulling the fly.

George Harvey Slack Leader

I have used Harvey leaders for most of my life, and I use the same leader for dry flies and nymphs with slight modifications. Clients who have never fished with this leader are amazed at the difference in performance. The formulas below are from *George Harvey: Memories, Patterns and Tactics* by Dan Shields (DLS Enterprises, 1998).

Standard Dry Fly Leader

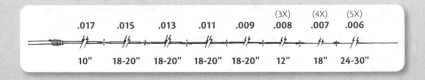

					(3X)	(4X)	(5X)
.017	.015	.013	.011	.009	.008	.007	.006
10"	18-20"	18-20"	18-20"	18-20"	12"	18"	24-30"

If I want to fish 6X tippet on the dry fly leader, I cut the 5X portion back to 18 inches and add 24 to 30 inches of 6X. Never fish less than 24 inches of tippet on a dry-fly rig.

Standard Nymph Leader

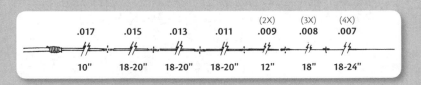

				(2X)	(3X)	(4X)
.017	.015	.013	.011	.009	.008	.007
10"	18-20"	18-20"	18-20"	12"	18"	18-24"

Use the same base leader as the dry-fly leader but cut the 2X back to 12 inches, and then attach 18 inches of 3X and 18 to 24 inches of 4X. If I need to fish lighter tippet, I cut the 4X to 18 inches and attach 18 to 24 inches of 5X.

For tying tippet to fly, I use a variation of the clinch knot, which I like to call the reverse clinch. Instead of attaching the clinch at the fly, I tie it back on the line and then pull it tight. This is one of the strongest knots I've ever seen, and I can tie it in the dark.

Nymph Rigs

Most of my nymphing rigs consist of two or more flies. Tandem rigs are more effective than single-fly rigs because you can cover multiple stages of a hatch, show the fish different species in a single drift, and can fish multiple depths.

Tangles will happen, whether we are fishing one or three flies, and I'll be the first to admit that it stinks to lose three flies when you hang up on bottom. But I'm on the water to fish, and I prefer to be aggressive rather than defensive in my approach to catching fish. If you're afraid of losing flies, than you probably aren't going to catch any fish, regardless of how many flies you have on. All states have rules on the number of flies you're allowed to fish with, so check your local game laws. For instance, in Pennsylvania, you can fish three flies, but in Montana, you're only allowed to fish two.

DROPPER AND TWO NYMPHS

My main nymph rig contains three types of flies: a fly with lots of movement, an attractor, and a standard nymph. The top fly is a soft hackle that imitates a moving insect and is tied off of a 4-inch tag end of a blood knot on 3X or 4X tippet. This pattern moves in the current and is most effective at the end of the drift as the rig either swings through the current or begins to rise in the current.

Next, I attach an attractor pattern, which is often a bead-head or weighted nymph, 12 to 18 inches below this fly with a reverse clinch. This pattern is designed to attract the trout's attention and

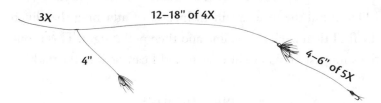

This is my standard nymphing rig, which allows me to cover multiple food items and multiple areas in the water column. I tie a soft hackle on the top dropper, a heavy attractor nymph in the middle, and a small suggestive nymph on the bottom. The last nymph on the rig is responsible for most catches, but all flies catch fish. Place split-shot below the soft hackle and the first nymph if needed.

get the rig deep. The final fly, and the real fish catcher, is tied on 6 to 8 inches of 4X or 5X off the bend of the attractor. This pattern is generally a small, drab nymph suggestive of whatever is hatching at the time. This last fly will be responsible for 90 percent of the fish caught on this rig.

The weight for this rig is placed between the dropper and the attractor. The distance between the dropper and attractor depends on water depth, usually approximately half the depth of the water. Why this rig works so well, I can only guess.

RIFFLE RIG

Another rig I like to use, especially in riffles, is two droppers tied off the main leader with the tag ends of blood knots and the third fly tied to the end of the tippet. I tie a weighted fly on the first dropper (the one closest to the angler), which gets the rig down in the skinny riffle water without having to use split-shot. This method allows for a better drift in riffles because the flies are free flowing and can ride the turbulent, up-and-down motion of the water the way that a natural insect would. If I need a little more weight, I'll put multiple weighted flies on the rig. Additionally, trout in this type of water often don't see every food item that drifts quickly through the current because of the turbulence in riffles. With the flies spaced equally at about 12 inches apart, you can cover a lot of the water column in a single drift.

MADISON RIG

I was introduced to the Woolly Bugger with a Copper John trailer years ago in Montana while fishing the Madison River. A few seasons ago, during some high water, I decided to give it a shot with a client, and the results were outstanding. Today, I use it any time the fishing gets tough, regardless of the conditions.

Tie a #14-16 Copper John to the bend of the Woolly Bugger's (#6-8) hook with about 8 to 12 inches of 4 or 5X tippet. Add split-shot above the Bugger. Dead-drift the flies in any water that you would normally nymph. The Woolly Bugger acts as an attractor, and you'll catch most fish on the nymph, even if you strip the Woolly Bugger back to you after the drift is over. You should also experiment with other streamer and nymph combinations.

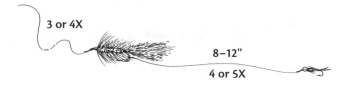

In the Madison rig, the large fly attracts a lot of attention and the small fly gets the fish. My favorite way to fish this rig is to dead-drift it with an occasional twitch. I then fish out the swing with a few small twitches before making another cast.

Dry-Fly Rigs

Trout that come to the surface to feed are often more discriminatory than when they feed under the surface. This not only tests our skill in delivering the pattern to the fish, it challenges our ability to pick the right combination of flies to fool the fish.

DRY AND DROPPER

One of my favorite ways to search the water is with a dry-dropper rig. My favorite pattern to use as a buoyant dry fly is a Royal Wulff. I enjoy tying them and they float like a cork, but the real advantage is that they catch fish. I can't explain it any better than the pattern's originator Lee Wulff did when he said, "Sometimes they want meat and potatoes, sometimes they want strawberry shortcake." I like to call it a glorified strike indicator that packs a punch. Because they are just that, a strike indicator, I tie them large, most often in sizes ranging from 8 to 12. I attach them to a leader terminating in 3X, and tie an attractor or bead-head off the bend, and then a nymph that matches whatever is hatching off of the bend of the attractor. The distance from the dry fly to the last

A dry fly and a dropper is one of the most effective ways of fishing a hatch because you can change the last fly to match what the fish are eating subsurface while using an indicator fly that imitates the dun.

nymph can vary from 12 inches to more than 48 inches, depending on the depth of the water.

During a hatch, I rarely fish a dropper longer than three feet and mostly fish unweighted flies that imitate different stages of an insect. Instead of a Royal Wulff, I choose a highly visible pattern that suggests the prevalent naturals. For example; during the Sulphur hatch I may choose a parachute dun pattern as the dry fly and tie one or two nymphs off the back of that to fish several different stages. I may begin, early in the hatch, by tying a Sulphur nymph on the dropper to suggest the many nymphs in the surface film that very often the trout key in on, and then change to a soft hackle or emerger pattern as the hatch progressed.

DRY AND DRY

As the hatch progresses and the spinner fall begins, I often tie a spinner to the bend of a parachute. Fishing dry flies in tandem is one of the best ways to cover a spinner fall for several reasons. First, many spinner falls occur when light is low, and the naturals are dainty little creatures that many times lie flush in the film. A parachute pattern with a visible post can be used as the indicator. Because it doesn't need to support any weight, as in the case of hanging a nymph off of a dry, it can be small, which reduces the chances of spooking fish at a time when the trout can be easily put down by an errant cast. Larger flies not only increase the chances of spooking fish, but because they are wind resistant you'll often find that the dropper pattern will land very close to the indicator fly, regardless of how much tippet you place in between the two flies. There is a good chance you will catch a fish on a small parachute during most spinner falls.

A small dry fly also makes a perfect indicator for a flush-floating spinner. I like to use at least 24 inches of tippet between two dry flies.

TIPPET AND DRIFT

The drift you are able to get with your dry-fly rig is often a result of how well the leader performs and how much slack is generated by the tippet. Most anglers don't use enough tippet, and often they use tippet that is too light. Personally, I would rather use 3 ½ feet of 4X than 2 feet of 5X. How much tippet you can handle depends on your casting ability, but I never use less than 24 inches, regardless of its diameter.

If your fly is buzzing across the surface right from the delivery and you can't build any slack into your leader, then you may need to extend or reduce the diameter of your tippet. A fly can twist and make a mess of tippet that is too light. If this happens, don't try to straighten the tippet—at that point it is already shot and weakened and it will go right back in a few more casts. Cut it off and use heavier tippet, but add two feet.

Chapter 11
Guide Flies

Trout flies are a big part of what makes fly fishing so much fun, and if you learn to wrap materials on a hook, there are no boundaries to your creative endeavors. Today, more than at any time in the history of fly fishing, there is more information available to fly tiers on just about any subject or material in existence. Consequently, we are in an age of fantastic fly tiers. Forty years ago, if you didn't know someone who tied flies, getting started could be difficult. Not only was it hard to find decent instruction, it was very difficult to find materials, much less good materials. All that has changed, and nearly half of the clients that I guide in central Pennsylvania tie their own flies. I have seen this change occur in only the last decade, and I see it as a step in a great direction for fly fishing.

Tying flies not only allows you to be more creative, and a little more self-sufficient in your fly fishing, but it also allows you to match the proportion, size, and colors of various stages of insects that you see on your home waters. This is where fly tying takes a turn from creative to scientific, and for those who enjoy matching the hatch, this takes fly fishing to a completely different level.

But, for all the amateur science and entomology involved in matching the hatch, sometimes on the stream anglers have to think outside the box. Occasionally, we get so wrapped up in the details of matching specific bugs, we forget that trout are just fish. And sometimes, fish will bite anything. Humans have a natural propensity to apply reason to all things, and if a trout eats a Purple Soft Hackle, there must have been cause for him to do so. Let me humbly submit, that sometimes they just bite, well . . . because.

I recently had dinner with Ann McIntosh and Charlie Meck, two dear friends that I have known for many years. Both are accomplished writers and world-class fishermen, and both, as you can well imagine, have incredible stories. On this particular evening, we were discussing some successful patterns that we like, and Charlie brought up the Green Weenie. Ann nearly jumped out of her seat and told Charlie, "You have to hear Eric and my Green Weenie story!"

It was late August on Spruce Creek in central Pennsylvania. The weather was hot, the sun was high, and the water was low and clear. I had Ann, who was then a client of mine, on this water because I had just recently leased it to use for my guiding, and I valued her opinion on the experience it delivered. The water had not been fished for years, and fortunately it had not been "managed" either, as so much of this well-known stream has, so it was a fairly wild piece of water. The population of trout was spread out, and the fish that we did see were large and spooky.

The game that day was small nymphs with very little weight. The slightest disturbance on the water caused by a poor cast or even split-shot sent the trout scurrying. We caught several fish, and Doug Lees, a friend of Ann's who was also fishing, had moved several fish as well. As we got to the top end of the property, I found a large brown feeding in a seam close to the bank. Ann and I watched him from a safe distance for a long time before we decided to cast to him. He was a beautiful trout, and I told Ann that we needed a picture of him for the website, so she had to catch him. We got into position well downstream of the trout, and Ann began casting.

We started with a single #16 Beadhead Pheasant Tail. (I was hesitant to even try a tandem rig because the trout that day had proved to be so spooky.) The fish continued to feed, even after Ann had put several excellent drifts right through its alley. We switched patterns and went with a #18 tan Beadhead Caddis Larva. Ann was handling the 12-foot leader perfectly, and I thought if the fish didn't take this pattern, I was going to go down to 6X tippet.

Drift after drift proved fruitless, and I decided to try a pattern without a bead and go down to 6X. The big brown continued to feed, a testament to Ann's skill, and I hesitantly switched the rig. For the record, I never nymph with 6X tippet, but this was an exceptional case. Drift after drift went right past the trout's nose, yet it continued to feed. In a last-ditch effort, I even tried a Trico nymph.

As this too proved to be nothing more than an exercise in casting, we took a break and Ann taught me some new cuss words. As we were sitting on the bank watching the fish continue to feed and I was asking Ann "How do you spell that?" Doug walked up and wondered what was going on. We pointed out the fish and told him everything we had tried. Ann was fed up by this point and told Doug to have at it.

Doug had a relatively large *Isonychia* nymph tied on and a Purple Soft Hackle. "Why not throw something bigger at this fish and see what he does," I said. Doug got into position and the pursuit started again, producing the exact same results. As our allotted time on the water began to run down, we were all resigned to the fact that sometimes you don't catch them. This was especially disturbing to me. I was still at a place in my life where I thought I could catch every fish on the planet (I've since grown up). I had tried everything I could think of. Or did I?

At the exact same time, Ann and I looked at each other and said, "We should throw a Weenie at that son-of-a-#%$&!" I quickly grabbed one out of my box and tied it on Doug's line. Chalk it up to being tired, frustrated, or just plain beaten, but Doug had no confidence in the plan, and his cast, which landed 8 feet from the fish, reflected this lack of faith. To my surprise, the big brown charged the Green Weenie as soon as it hit the water. Doug landed the fish and we all stood there shocked. The picture was on my website for years, and the story will always be of value. Just when you think you know what you're doing in this sport, you'll see something like this that will make you wonder what you really do know.

But despite this, my day-to-day experience has been that presentation is more important than pattern selection—though there are always exceptions to keep us on our toes, which the Weenie story proves. I carry at least a thousand flies with me when I'm guiding, but I will probably never use two-thirds of them. I have found over the years that the answer is more often how I'm doing it, not what I'm doing it with. This belief has narrowed the selection of flies that I use considerably. Any guide will undoubtedly carry more than he needs. It's the nature of the business. These days though, I find myself replacing the same patterns over and over, rather than adding new ones to my boxes.

Fly patterns can be realistic, impressionistic, or attractors. When I say realistic, I'm not talking about the realistic mating crickets that you see the guys tying at the shows. Those are works of art, but they're not fishing flies. I'm talking about patterns that very closely resemble natural insects. These are important patterns to carry with you and everyone should have some of these in their boxes for specific purposes. Some hatches on a trout stream require you to match exactly what is going on.

For example, anglers that have specific imitations of the nymph, emerger, dun, and spinner stages for the Sulphur hatch in central Pennsylvania will do much better than they would with generic Pheasant Tails, imported parachute patterns, and generic Rusty Spinners. Prolific hatches such as this one require close imitations, and while you may achieve some success with generic patterns early in the hatch, you will be sorely disappointed a week later once the hatch is in full swing.

Impressionistic patterns are often generic, but their built-in movement and shape suggest many types of insects, and I probably carry more of this type of fly than any other. Nymphs such as Hare's Ears, Pheasant Tails, and generic caddis larvae that I carry are good examples of impressionistic patterns. Dry flies such as the Adams and the Elk-Hair Caddis are not imitations of any specific mayfly or caddis, but their general shape and color suggests many different species that I might encounter onstream.

Attractor patterns may have an overall shape that represents food, but they usually incorporate elements that trigger a strike from the trout. The Wulff series of dry flies comes to mind. They have an overall shape of many mayfly patterns, yet the peacock herl and red floss rib do not match any mayfly. Yet, the trout can't seem to help themselves. Charlie Meck's Patriot is another fine example. The body of this fly is tied with smolt-blue Krystal Flash, and although there are no bright blue mayflies in existence, trout love to eat the Patriot. Attractors are an important part of our fishing. When I guide in Montana, nearly every fly we use is an attractor. Those fish have a short growing season and need to eat. Each year when I come home, I recommit to fishing more Wulffs, Copper Johns, and buggy nymphs with rubber legs. These flies often produce when nothing else will.

There are many variables that go into pattern selection, including time of year, water depth, clarity, current speed, and behavior or location of the insect or other food you are imitating. Even when insects are hatching and you have the benefit of seeing what bug to imitate, you still must consider the behavior of the insect when selecting a pattern and deciding how to fish it. How is the insect behaving? Where is the trout taking the insect? Is the insect moving, as in the case of a caddis skittering across the surface? Is the nymph stuck in the meniscus while hatching? These are all issues that come into play when trying to decide what fly to tie onto the end of our tippet.

Close visual observation can uncover clues as to what's happening, but often we are unable to see the many tiny intricacies that occur on a trout stream. To make selecting a fly easier, I recommend increasing your odds and prospecting with two flies. In Pennsylvania, we can fish three flies at once, but some states limit the number of flies to two. But I always like to fish multiple patterns to increase my chances, whether fishing dry and dropper or multiple nymphs in cooler water temperatures. I typically use a pattern to attract the trouts' attention, and tie a smaller pattern that is a closer representative of a natural insect off of it.

I determine the natural pattern that I am going to fish based on my years of experience on my local streams, coupled with on-stream observation, which is critical—even more so if you are new to a particular piece of water. You must use your powers of observation. Get into the river and pick up some rocks. You don't need to know the Latin names of the bugs, nor do you need to know what they are. If you find a lot of brown nymphs that are a size 16, there is your starting point.

If you're only fishing one pattern, and do not know exactly what the fish are feeding on, I recommend using an impressionistic pattern that you have confidence in. Whether you chose to fish the surface or underneath it, a pattern that suggests more than one type of food will give you the best opportunity for success.

Confidence also plays a large role in pattern selection. Over the years, I have found myself using fewer patterns and fishing those that I believe in more efficiently. The following patterns are some of my favorites, and I would never be on the stream without them.

Walt's Worm

Hook: #10-16 Mustad 9671
Weight: .015-inch-diameter lead wire covering the hook shank
Thread: Gray 6/0
Body: Hare's Ear Plus #1 (Natural Hare's Ear)

This pattern was developed for central Pennsylvania's Spring Creek in the early 1970s by my good friend Walt Young. It has since become extremely popular on all of the state's streams, and most anyone from Pennsylvania will have a few of these in their box. I have caught fish on this pattern in every state I have ever fished in. When Walt ties this pattern at the shows, he apologizes for its simplicity and says, "I'm sorry folks, I wish I could make it more complicated than this."

I fish this pattern year-round, often as a heavily weighted attractor in my nymph rig. I like to use a #10 to dredge turbulent water and deep runs (in the large sizes, I cover the hook shank with lead and then double it back over), though smaller or unweighted versions work well for shallower water or tailouts. The Walt's Worm is probably best used as a crane fly larva but can also pass for a scud, caddis, or shrimp. Almost all trout streams have crane flies in them, and the larvae are familiar food for trout.

Ginger Nymph

Hook: #12-18 Mustad 3906B
Weight: .005- to .010-inch-
diameter lead wire
Thread: Tan 6/0
Tail: Hen pheasant fibers
Rib: Fine gold wire
Body: Ginger Hare-Tron
Thorax: Dark brown squirrel
dubbing
Legs: Hen pheasant fibers

The Ginger Nymph is a pattern similar to one that Joe Humphreys uses for the Sulphur nymph. This pattern is buggy, and the gold wire rib gives the pattern a translucency by creating an inner core of solid color underneath the saturated dubbing. This fly represents one of three major colors that I believe are key in imitating mayfly nymphs, along with brown and olive. It produces results all year long, in all water types (not just those with Sulphur hatches).

Olive Nymph

Hook:	#14-20 Mustad 3906B
Weight:	.005- to .010-inch-diameter lead wire
Thread:	Olive 6/0
Tail:	Pheasant tail fibers
Rib:	Fine gold wire
Body:	Olive squirrel dubbing
Wing Case:	Black or brown poly
Thorax:	Olive squirrel dubbing

This generic pattern can be tied in several shades of olive to match a lot of different nymphs. I do particularly well with it during the early season and late fall. In sizes 14 to 18, this is my go-to pattern anytime Blue-Winged Olives are in the air. I fish this pattern most often in a size 16, but larger sizes will imitate many of the larger mayflies during the seasons when they are not close to hatching. At this time they are often drab in color, and you can't go wrong with olive. I often fish this pattern either high on the rig hanging off the dropper or as the last fly.

**Bead-Head
Caddis Larva**

Hook: #12-20 Daiichi 1120
Thread: Black 6/0
Rib: Fine gold or silver wire
Body: Tan dubbing
Legs: Hen feather fibers
Thorax: Peacock herl

Caddis are the predominate species of insect in the watersheds that I fish, and I use this pattern year-round as the bottom fly for fishing in the riffles, where caddis are common. This easy-to-tie pattern is very effective in green, tan, gray, olive, white, and brown. Bright green or chartreuse and orange are also effective colors. In central Pennsylvania, bright colors always seem to fish well in the early season, and the drab colors produce better later in the year. Pick colors to match your local species.

Mega-Prince

Hook:	#8-14 Mustad 9671
Bead:	Tungsten
Weight:	.015-inch-diameter lead wire
Thread:	Black 6/0
Tail:	Brown goose biots
Rib:	Fine gold wire
Body:	Peacock herl
Wings:	White goose biots
Legs:	Dark or natural CDC

Lance Wilt, one of the best young guides in the business, introduced me to this pattern while we were fishing Montana's Ruby River. The Prince Nymph has always been an effective trout catcher, but the addition of a few turns of CDC behind the bead makes this pattern even more deadly. It has everything trout love—peacock herl, white wings, and CDC.

I fish this pattern in the middle of the tandem rig, where I like the heaviest fly, when the water is slightly high or off color, but have caught fish with it all times. I use this pattern sometimes as the only weight on the rig, and it can be a great way to get deep quickly in a heavy current. This fly is a big-fish producer.

Zebra Midge

Hook: #16-20 Daiichi 1130
Bead: Tungsten or glass bead
Thread: Black 6/0 or 8/0
Rib: Fine gold or silver wire
Body: Tying thread

This is yet another extremely simple, but deadly, pattern. If nymphing, I fish this pattern on a dropper at the top of a multiple-fly rig, but more often than not, I use this pattern as a dropper off of a dry fly. When you come across a finicky trout that you just can't figure out, hang this pattern from a caddis and hold on. Midges are an important part of a trout's diet, and they hatch all year long, but I use this pattern most when the fishing gets tough during the heat of summer and into fall, especially for sporadic risers. You'll want to have a variety of sizes and colors such as black, brown, tan, gray, white, olive, green, and red.

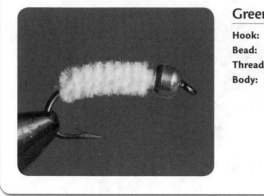

Green Weenie

Hook: #10-16 Mustad 9671
Bead: Gold
Thread: Chartreuse 6/0
Body: Chartreuse chenille (small)

I'm not exactly sure what it is supposed to imitate—some say caddis or inchworms—but regardless, it has saved the day on more than one occasion. I fish this pattern on the bottom of the water column, so in the tandem, it would be either the weighted attractor or the point fly, which I hang off of the weighted attractor. This is determined by size. If I use a large Green Weenie, it becomes the weight, and a smaller one becomes the point. I most often fish this fly with a gold bead or weighted heavily with lead wire to get it down in swiftly moving water or deep pools. My favorite time to fish the Green Weenie is around the edges of the hatch season—early spring, midsummer, and in the fall. As easy as this one is to tie, everyone should have a few.

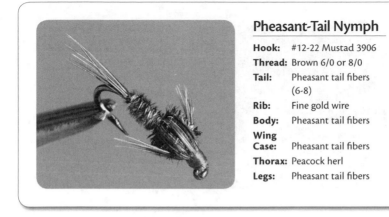

Pheasant-Tail Nymph

Hook: #12-22 Mustad 3906
Thread: Brown 6/0 or 8/0
Tail: Pheasant tail fibers (6-8)
Rib: Fine gold wire
Body: Pheasant tail fibers
Wing Case: Pheasant tail fibers
Thorax: Peacock herl
Legs: Pheasant tail fibers

This pattern represents most mayfly nymphs, and if I were only able to pick one imitation to fish under the surface, this would be it. When I'm fishing a Pheasant Tail, it is usually in the point position on the bottom, or as the top nymph on a dropper. Its shape represents a dislodged, swimming, or crawling nymph, and trout will pick this pattern up regardless of where it is in the current. I rarely tie these patterns with weight because I often fish them higher in the water column as an emerger, though a bead on this pattern makes it a terrific dropper for a dry fly. You can fish this pattern in all water types, on any water, and at any time of year.

Sulphur Nymph

Hook: #14-18 Mustad 3906B
Thread: Ginger 6/0 or 8/0
Tail: Wood duck
Rib: Amber V-Rib
Body: Natureblend Dubbing
#12 (Cinnamon)
**Wing
Case:** Black poly
Thorax: Same dubbing as body

The Sulphur hatch is one of the hatches where you must match the natural. The color of the nymphs (and duns) varies, so inspect the naturals in your home water. I have found this particular pattern very effective in central Pennsylvania. The key to its success is the black wing case. When Sulphurs are close to hatching, their wing cases turn very dark, and I believe this is a trigger for the trout.

I begin fishing this pattern within a month of the hatch, as the nymphs become active. Sulphur nymphs are so prevalent in our waters that we could fish this pattern year-round with success, but for most of the year, they are a brown to olive color, which is covered by some of the other nymphs in the text. I fish this pattern most often on the point, or higher in the water column off a dropper. I don't weight it so that I can fish it in the film as an emerger. This pattern has probably caught more big fish for me over the years than any other.

LaFontaine Deep Sparkle Pupa

Hook:	#12-18 Mustad 3906B
Weight:	.015-inch-diameter lead wire
Thread:	Black 6/0 or 8/0
Case:	Antron tied in at bend of hook and pulled over to thorax
Body:	Dark brown squirrel dubbing
Legs:	Pheasant tail fibers

Gary LaFontaine got it right when he developed this pattern. This fly is one of the most effective subsurface patterns I have ever fished, regardless of whether caddis are in the air. Caddis are such a prevalent species that the trout are used to seeing them and will always eat it. The right Antron for this pattern is hard to find. Try buying pure Antron dubbing from Wapsi and separate the fibers out and use that. It makes a better air bubble.

CDC Caddis

Hook: #12-20 Mustad 94840
Thread: Black 6/0 or 8/0
Body: Dark brown Superfine
Hackle: Natural CDC
Wing: Natural deer hair

This generic pattern is designed to imitate any caddis fly by changing the size and color. The CDC wrapped as a collar around the thorax area extends beyond the hook bend and moves in the current so enticingly that I have abandoned the old elk-hair patterns for this one. Caddis on the surface are in constant motion. This pattern imitates the movement without the angler having to do anything. Additionally, as the CDC becomes wet, the abdomen naturally dips the into the film, making a perfect emerger. I have even fished this pattern wet and done extremely well. Do not use liquid floatant on CDC as it will destroy the structure of the feather. When this fly gets fish slime on it or completely soaked, I simply squeeze it in a paper towel and it's ready to fish again. After squeezing the water from the fly, you can treat it with Frog's Fanny or any similar desiccant.

Adams Parachute

Hook: #10-22 Mustad 94840
Thread: Gray 6/0 or 8/0
Tail: Grizzly and brown hackle fibers, mixed
Body: Adams gray Superfine
Post: White calf body hair
Hackle: Grizzly and brown, mixed

This standard-issue fly pattern represents dozens of natural insects on most trout streams throughout the country, and will be productive in all sizes at various times during the season to imitate any of the dark mayflies. The small to medium sizes represent Paraleps (Blue Quills), *Baetis*, and midges, while larger sizes imitate insects like the Slate Drakes and Gray Drakes. I often go to the Adams Parachute when I'm having trouble catching rising fish, and it is often the answer.

Royal Wulff

Hook: #8-14 Mustad 94840

Thread: Black 6/0 or 8/0

Wing: White calf tail

Tail: Brown calf tail

Rib: Fine gold wire

Body: Peacock herl with a midrib of red floss

Hackle: Dark brown hackle

This is one of my favorite patterns to fish, and the only pattern I use for brook trout. I use this pattern most often as a glorified strike indicator, but catch a lot of trout on it. Lee Wulff said, "Sometimes they want meat and potatoes, sometimes they want strawberry shortcake." My experiences with this pattern over the years have given me an appreciation for a trout's fondness for certain colors and general buggyness in a fly. I have caught trout with this pattern consistently on some of the toughest, most technical streams in the eastern United States when there was nothing else they would eat. Sometimes dessert is more appealing than the main course.

Peacock & Furnace Soft Hackle

Hook: #10-18 Mustad 3906B
Thread: Black 6/0 or 8/0
Rib: Fine gold wire
Body: Peacock herl
Hackle: Furnace hen

This is one of the oldest fly patterns in existence. It has lasted centuries for good reason. First of all, any fly with peacock herl is effective. Add the movement of a soft hen feather on it and it makes it that much better. This pattern is a good representation of many living things that inhabit trout streams. I use it most often during caddis hatches, particularly the Grannom hatch. There is rarely a time when I'm nymphing that I don't have a soft hackle on the line somewhere if bugs are hatching. I fish the Peacock & Furnace most often off the dropper but have had success fishing it right on the bottom as well. This pattern works well in all water types, but fishes particularly well in turbulent water.

Purple Soft Hackle

Hook:	#10-14 Daiichi 1260
Thread:	Black 6/0 or 8/0
Tail:	Dark dun hen
Rib:	Fine silver wire
Body:	Blended purple dubbing
Thorax:	Peacock herl
Hackle:	Dark dun hen

This fly was a concoction that Skip Galbraith and I came up with for the *Isonychia* on the Little Juniata River in central Pennsylvania. Its success was incredible, particularly in the fall. One day I watched Skip break off three fish in a row, on 3X tippet. We began to tie this pattern commercially, and I started to fish it year-round with success. Today, I'm never without at least a few of these patterns in my box.

Isonychia mayflies are known to crawl to the rocks on the banks of the stream and hatch from the edge of a dry rock. While this is very common, and you will see hundreds of shucks on the rocks each day, they also hatch out of the water, which this pattern imitates. I fish it most often in the fall of the year in riffles and tailouts. I fish it off of the top dropper with 3X tippet, because the take is often violent.

Sulphur Soft Hackle

Hook:	#12-16 Daiichi 1260
Thread:	Yellow 6/0 or 8/0
Tail:	Light- to medium-dun hen fibers
Rib:	Yellow DMC single-strand floss
Body:	Yellow Superfine
Thorax:	Rust or burnt orange squirrel dubbing
Hackle:	Light- to medium-dun hen hackle

This pattern has caught more fish for me during the Sulphurs than any other single pattern I've ever fished. During the month-long hatch, I fish this pattern deep when I'm nymphing during the day. I'll often hang it off the dropper or fish it on the point at various times, and when the bugs hatch in the evening, I fish it in the film behind a dun. Whether the trout take it for an emerger, struggling dun, or spinner, this pattern matches every stage of the Sulphur hatch once emergence begins. Keep the body of this fly sparse. This pattern can be effective for all of the light-colored mayflies, and holds an important place in my box.

Pheasant-Tail Soft Hackle

Hook: #12-20 Mustad 3906
Thread: Brown 6/0 or 8/0
Tail: Pheasant tail fibers
Rib: Fine gold wire
Body: Pheasant tail fibers
Thorax: Peacock herl
Hackle: Partridge

This pattern is a great imitation of a dislodged or hatching nymph. The partridge feather moves and breathes with the current, and pheasant tail is not only a perfect color for most nymphs but the fibers have thousands of tiny barbules that move and breathe with the current, suggesting life. The partridge hen hackle adds to the movement of this pattern, and its general shape and appearance is so suggestive, trout can't ignore it. I fish this pattern year-round on a dropper, above two nymphs, in all water types.

Hare's-Ear Soft Hackle

Hook: #10-20 Mustad 3906
Thread: Tan 6/0 or 8/0
Tail: Hare's mask guard hairs
Rib: Copper wire
Body: Clipped underfur from hare's mask
Thorax: Clipped hair from hare's mask
Hackle: Partridge

This pattern is a great imitation of many of the burrowing nymphs like the Green and Brown Drakes. It is a meaty and buggy fly that trout cannot resist because of the built-in movement of the soft hackle and buggy dubbing. I love to fish this pattern in the riffles where I think it may be a good representation of stoneflies as well as emerging caddis. I fish this pattern on the point (bottom) most often and find it particularly effective on the swing, at the end of the drift. I use this pattern at all times during the year, though it is particularly effective during the late spring/early summer when many of the drakes begin to hatch. Smaller sizes are very productive in riffles, any time of year, but especially during caddis hatches.

Olive Soft Hackle

Hook: #14-20 Mustad 3906B
Thread: Olive 6/0 or 8/0
Tail: Medium-dun hen fibers
Rib: Fine gold wire
Body: Olive Superfine
Thorax: Brown squirrel dubbing
Hackle: Medium dun hen

Blue-Winged Olives are one of the most important hatches across the country, so patterns to imitate them are essential. There are only a few months out of the year when Olives aren't present on the streams that I fish the most, and this pattern will take fish 12 months out of the year. I most often fish it off of a dropper if I'm nymphing, or hang it off of a dry fly when fishing on the surface. This pattern is most effective as an emerger fished within the top few inches of the water column. Tie it sparsely to imitate the natural, and use a dubbing color to match your local insects.

Spinner Soft Hackle

Hook: #14-16 Daiichi 1260
Thread: Rust 6/0 or 8/0
Tail: Light dun hen fibers
Rib: Tan DMC single-strand floss
Body: Rust Superfine (lightly dubbed)
Thorax: Rust Superfine
Hackle: Light dun hen hackle

This pattern was my answer to a frustrating evening on the Sulphur spinners one night a few years ago. It has become my go-to pattern during tough, technical spinner falls when matching the naturals can be extremely tough because of their size or movement. This pattern can also be very effective when fished on the bottom through a heavy riffle or run. Many spinners get washed into these areas and are drowned by heavy water. However, I most often hang it off of a visible dun pattern and even the most finicky trout will take this pattern with a vengeance.

Rusty Spinner

Hook:	#12-22 Mustad 94840
Thread:	Rust 6/0 or 8/0
Tail:	Light to medium dun hackle fibers
Rib:	Tan DMC single-strand floss
Body:	Rust Superfine (lightly dubbed)
Thorax:	Brown Superfine
Wing:	Light dun colored poly

This is an essential spinner pattern that will cover all of your imitation needs by changing the color and size. Proportion is key. Most of the spinners we fish are too big, or the wings are too heavy or short. If you buy your spinners, they are probably not proportioned correctly unless they are tied by a local tier. Take some time the next time you're on the water during a spinner fall and compare your imitation to a natural. More than likely, the body of the natural will be much thinner that our imitation. Mayfly spinners are dainty little creatures and in most cases, if we dub a body onto a spinner pattern, it's going to be larger than the natural. I think this is more detrimental with the spinner than with a dun because there are millions of them lying still on the water that the fish can scrutinize. Fill your fly boxes with a selection of sizes that will cover all the hatches.

Sulphur Dun

Hook: #14-18 Mustad 94840
Thread: Yellow 6/0 or 8/0
Tail: Light dun hackle fibers
Rib: Yellow DMC single-strand floss
Wing: Hen feather tips (rounded)
Hackle: Light dun hackle

The Sulphur hatch can produce some of the most technical fishing of the season. This pattern has been the answer on more than one occasion for me and my clients. It features a strong wing profile that is quite often the difference maker when everyone else on the river is throwing parachutes.

Evening Sulphur hatches in mid-May in the Northeast are often cool, drizzly events. This can spell trouble for the Sulphur duns trying to dry their wings and reach the safe haven of the stream's forested edges. Duns will ride the surface for long periods of time, sitting motionless with their wings perched like miniature sailboats. Anglers dream of just such conditions and the trout are shown every pattern under the sun. This is one that I've had success with under all conditions, especially later in the hatch.

Olive Parachute

Hook: #16-22 Mustad 94840
Thread: Olive 8/0
Tail: Dark dun hackle fibers
Rib: Olive DMC single-strand floss
Body: Olive Superfine
Post: Light dun poly
Hackle: Dark dun hackle

Blue-Winged Olives (BWOs) are an important species on trout streams all over the country. Some of the best, most memorable days I have ever had on a trout stream were the result of incredible Blue-Winged Olive hatches. Though they often happen during the foulest weather, BWOs will almost always bring trout to the surface. I choose to use a pattern that is highly visible and will continue to float despite the elements. This parachute pattern features a light dun post, yet is still visible on the surface in low light conditions.

Griffith's Gnat

Hook: #18-24 Mustad 94840
Thread: Black 8/0
Body: Peacock herl
Hackle: Grizzly hackle

This is possibly one of the most simplistic, effective patterns of all. All too often, we encounter trout eating midges that we can barely see. I have watched anglers frustrate themselves trying to match the hatch in these situations before they resorted to trying this old standby. When the trout are on the little stuff, this pattern will almost always fool them. Designed to imitate a cluster of midges, this pattern leaves little more than the tips of its hackle in the surface film, the same way that the naturals do.

Index

Index